Dear Future Exam Success Story:

Congratulations on your purchase of our study guide. Our goal in writing our study guide was to cover the content on the test, as well as provide insight into typical test taking mistakes and how to overcome them.

Standardized tests are a key component of being successful, which only increases the importance of doing well in the high-pressure high-stakes environment of test day. How well you do on this test will have a significant impact on your future, and we have the research and practical advice to help you execute on test day.

The product you're reading now is designed to exploit weaknesses in the test itself, and help you avoid the most common errors test takers frequently make.

How to use this study guide

We don't want to waste your time. Our study guide is fast-paced and fluff-free. We suggest going through it a number of times, as repetition is an important part of learning new information and concepts.

First, read through the study guide completely to get a feel for the content and organization. Read the general success strategies first, and then proceed to the content sections. Each tip has been carefully selected for its effectiveness.

Second, read through the study guide again, and take notes in the margins and highlight those sections where you may have a particular weakness.

Finally, bring the manual with you on test day and study it before the exam begins.

Your success is our success

We would be delighted to hear about your success. Send us an email and tell us your story. Thanks for your business and we wish you continued success.

Sincerely,

Mometrix Test Preparation Team

Need more help? Check out our flashcards at: http://MometrixFlashcards.com/ISEE

TABLE OF CONTENTS

Top 20 Test Taking Tips

1. Carefully follow all the test registration procedures
2. Know the test directions, duration, topics, question types, how many questions
3. Setup a flexible study schedule at least 3-4 weeks before test day
4. Study during the time of day you are most alert, relaxed, and stress free
5. Maximize your learning style; visual learner use visual study aids, auditory learner use auditory study aids
6. Focus on your weakest knowledge base
7. Find a study partner to review with and help clarify questions
8. Practice, practice, practice
9. Get a good night's sleep; don't try to cram the night before the test
10. Eat a well balanced meal
11. Know the exact physical location of the testing site; drive the route to the site prior to test day
12. Bring a set of ear plugs; the testing center could be noisy
13. Wear comfortable, loose fitting, layered clothing to the testing center; prepare for it to be either cold or hot during the test
14. Bring at least 2 current forms of ID to the testing center
15. Arrive to the test early; be prepared to wait and be patient
16. Eliminate the obviously wrong answer choices, then guess the first remaining choice
17. Pace yourself; don't rush, but keep working and move on if you get stuck
18. Maintain a positive attitude even if the test is going poorly
19. Keep your first answer unless you are positive it is wrong
20. Check your work, don't make a careless mistake

Verbal Reasoning

Synonyms

As part of your exam, you need to understand how words connect to each other. This is done with understanding words that mean the same thing or synonyms. For example, *dry* and *arid* are synonyms. There are pairs of words in English that can be called synonyms. Yet, they have somewhat different definitions.

For example, *wise* and *intelligent* can be used to describe someone who is very educated. So, you would be correct to call them synonyms. However, *wise* is used for good judgment. *Intelligent* is closer to good thinking.

Words should not be called synonyms when their differences are too great. For example, *hot* and *warm* are not synonyms because their meanings are too different. How do you know when two words are synonyms? First, try to replace one word for the other word. Then, be sure that the meaning of the sentence has not changed. Replacing *warm* for *hot* in a sentence gives a different meaning. *Warm* and *hot* may seem close in meaning. Yet, *warm* means that the temperature is normal. And, *hot* means that the temperature is very high.

> ➢ **Review Video:** Synonyms and Antonyms
> *Visit* ***mometrix.com/academy*** *and enter* ***Code:*** **105612**

Synonyms

For the Synonyms section, you will have one word and four choices for a synonym of that word. Before you look at the choices, try to think of a few words that could be a synonym for your question. Then, check the choices for a synonym of the question. Some words may seem close to the question, but you are looking for the best choice of a synonym. So, don't let your first reaction be your final decision.

Example 1
Precise:

A. Focus
B. Careless
C. Exact
D. Costly

Example 2
Fringe:

A. Neglect
B. Margin
C. Fade
D. Center

<u>Example 3</u>
Splendid:

A. Unknown
B. Beautiful
C. Awkward
D. Ordinary

Answers
Example 1: C, Exact
Example 2: B, Margin
Example 3: B, Beautiful

Sentence Completion

On your exam and in everyday life, you will be introduced to unfamiliar words. Most of the time, the definition of an unknown word can be learned from context clues. Context refers to how a word or phrase is used in a sentence. Understanding the context can help you decide which word or phrase should go in the blank. There are different contextual clues such as definition, description, example, comparison, and contrast. The following are examples:
- Definition: the unknown word is clearly defined by the previous words.
  "When he was painting, his instrument was a __." (paintbrush)
- Description: the unknown word is described by the previous words.
  "I was hot, tired, and thirsty; I was __." (dehydrated)
- Example: the unknown word is part of a series of examples.
  "Water, soda, and __ were the offered beverages." (coffee)
- Comparison: the unknown word is compared to another word.
  "Barney is agreeable and happy like his __ parents." (positive)
- Contrast: the unknown word is contrasted with another word.
  "I prefer cold weather to __ conditions." (hot)

Sentence Completion

The second type of question in the Verbal Reasoning section asks you to read a sentence with a missing word and fill in the blank with the appropriate word. Also, some questions will ask you to read part of a sentence, and you will need to decide how to finish the sentence. In the same way with the Synonyms section, you should read the question and think of a few possible ways to complete the sentence. Then, look over your choices and select the best choice.

<u>Example 1</u>
Determine how to complete this sentence:

       Danny was so _____ that his teacher had to keep reminding him to be serious.

To fill in the blank, you need to look at the context of the sentence. In this example, Danny's teacher reminds him to be serious. If the teacher has to remind Danny to be serious, then Danny must be doing the opposite. When someone is not being serious, they are being silly or causing mischief. Then, you would look over your answer choices and decide on a word that is similar to being silly or causing mischief.

<u>Example 2</u>
Determine how to complete this sentence:

       As an actor, he _____ a king, a homeless man, and an investigator.

In this example, you know that the subject of the sentence is an actor. So, you would look over your answer choices and decide on a word that relates to acting like *portrayed* or *represented*.

<u>Example 3</u>
Determine how to complete this sentence:

       When the commander arrived at the base, the soldiers _____.

In this example, we see the connection between soldiers and their commanding officer. You do not need to know the rules and procedures of greeting someone of a high military rank. The soldiers are not as important as the commander. So, you will be looking for an answer choice that has the soldiers showing respect to the commander. An example could be "the soldiers took their position" or "the soldiers saluted their officer."

Mathematics

Number Sense

Numbers and their Classifications

There are several different kinds of numbers. When you learn to count as a child, you start with *Natural Numbers*. You may know them as counting numbers. These numbers begin with 1, 2, 3, and so on. *Whole Numbers* are all natural numbers and zero.

Aside from the number 1, all natural numbers are known as prime or composite. *Prime Numbers* are natural numbers that are greater than 1 and have factors that are 1 and itself (e.g., 3). On the other hand, *Composite Numbers* are natural numbers that are greater than 1 and are not prime numbers. The number 1 is a special case because it is not a prime number or composite number.

Numbers are the basic building blocks of mathematics. These terms show some elements of numbers:

Even number – Any integer that can be divided by 2 and does not leave a remainder. Example: 2, 4, 6, 8, etc.

Odd number – Any integer that cannot be divided evenly by 2. For example: 3, 5, 7, 9, and so on.

Decimal number – a number that uses a decimal point to show the part of the number that is less than one. Example: 1.234.

Decimal point – a symbol used to separate the ones place from the tenths place in decimals. This symbol is used to separate dollars from cents in currency.

Decimal place – the position of a number to the right of the decimal point. In the decimal 0.123, the 1 is in the first place to the right of the decimal point. This is the place for tenths. The 2 is in the second place. This is the place for hundredths. The 3 is in the third place. This is the place for thousandths.

The decimal, or base 10, system is a number system that uses ten different digits (0, 1, 2, 3, 4, 5, 6, 7, 8, 9). Another system is the binary, or base 2, number system. This system is used by computers and uses the numbers 0 and 1. Some think that the base 10 system started because people had only their 10 fingers for counting.

Place Value

Write the place value of each digit in the following number: 14,059.826

>   1: ten thousands
>   4: thousands
>   0: hundreds
>   5: tens
>   9: ones
>   8: tenths
>   2: hundredths
>   6: thousandths

Writing Numbers in Word Form

Example 1
Write each number in words.

29: twenty-nine
478: four hundred seventy-eight
9,435: nine thousand four hundred thirty-five
98,542: ninety-eight thousand five hundred forty-two
302, 876: three hundred two thousand eight hundred seventy-six

Example 2
Write each decimal in words.

0.06: six hundredths
0.6: six tenths
6.0: six

0.009: nine thousandths;
0.113: one hundred thirteen thousandths;
0.901: nine hundred and one thousandths

The Number Line
A number line is a graph to see the distance between numbers. Basically, this graph shows the relationship between numbers. So, a number line may have a point for zero and may show negative numbers on the left side of the line. Also, any positive numbers are placed on the right side of the line. Before you work with negative numbers, you need to understand absolute values. Basically, a number's *Absolute Value* is the distance away from zero that a number is on the number line. The absolute value of a number is always positive and is written as $|x|$. If a number like -4 is added with a +2, then the sum is -2. So, the absolute value of $|-2|$ is +2.

Example 1: Name each point on the number line below:

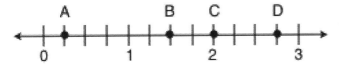

Use the dashed lines on the number line to identify each point. Each dashed line between two whole numbers is $\frac{1}{4}$. The line halfway between two numbers is $\frac{1}{2}$.

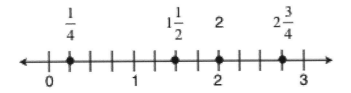

➤ **Review Video:** <u>Numbers and Their Classification</u>
*Visit **mometrix.com/academy** and enter **Code: 461071***

Listing Numbers: Least to Greatest

<u>Example 1</u>
4,002; 280; 108,511; 9

Answer: 9; 280; 4,002; 108,511

<u>Example 2</u>
5,075,000,600; 190,800,330; 7,000,300,001

Answer: 190,800,330; 5,075,000,600; 7,000,300,001

Operations and Properties

Operations

There are four basic operations in math: addition, subtraction, multiplication, and division.

Addition increases the value of one number by the value of another number. Example: 2 + 4 = 6; 8 + 9 = 17. The result is called the sum. With addition, the order does not matter. 4 + 2 or 2 + 4 equals 6. This is the commutative property for addition.

Subtraction decreases the value of one number by the value of another number. The result is called the difference. Example: 6 – 4 = 2 and 17 – 8 = 9. Note for subtraction that the order does matter. For example, 6 – 4 and 4 – 6 do not have the same difference.

Multiplication is like repeated addition. This operation tells how many times one number needs to be added to the other number. Example: 3 × 2 (three times two) = 2 + 2 + 2 = 6. With multiplication, the order does not matter. 2 × 3 (or 3 + 3) = 3 × 2 (or 2 + 2 + 2). This is the commutative property for multiplication.

Division is the opposite operation to multiplication. This operation shows how much of a number is in another number. The first number is known as the dividend. The second number is known as the divisor. The answer to the division problem is known as the quotient.

Example: $20 \div 4 = 5$. If 20 is split into 4 equal parts, then each part is 5. With division, the order of the numbers does matter. $20 \div 4$ and $4 \div 20$ do not give the same result. Note that you cannot divide a number by zero. If you try to divide a number by zero, then the answer is known as undefined.

Order of Operations

Order of Operations is a list of rules that gives the order of doing each operation in an expression. If you have an expression that with many different operations, Order of Operations tells you which operations to do first. An easy way to remember Order of Operations is PEMDAS.

This is written out as "Please Excuse My Dear Aunt Sally." PEMDAS stands for Parentheses, Exponents, Multiplication, Division, Addition, Subtraction. You need to understand that multiplication and division are equal as steps. Also, addition and subtraction are equal as steps. So, those pairs of operations are worked from left to right.

Example: Use order of operations for the expression $5 + 20 \div 4 \times (2 + 3)^2 - 6$.
P: Work on the operations inside the parentheses, $(2 + 3) = 5$.
E: Simplify the exponents, $(5)^2 = 25$.
The equation now looks like this: $5 + 20 \div 4 \times 25 - 6$.
MD: Work on multiplication and division from left to right, $20 \div 4 = 5$; then $5 \times 25 = 125$.
The equation now looks like this: $5 + 125 - 6$.
AS: Work on addition and subtraction from left to right, $5 + 125 = 130$; then $130 - 6 = 124$.

> ➢ **Review Video:** <u>Order of Operations</u>
> *Visit **mometrix.com/academy** and enter **Code: 259675***

Properties

The Commutative Property of Addition is shown here, which states that you can add terms in any order.
$$2x + y = y + 2x$$

The Distributive Property is shown here, which states that a number multiplied to an expression in parentheses must be multiplied to every term in the parentheses.
$$5 \times (x + 1) = (5 \times x) + (5 \times 1)$$

The Identity Property of Multiplication is shown here, which states that multiplying a number or term by 1 does not change its value.
$$3 \times 1 = 3$$

The Commutative Property of Multiplication is shown here, which states that you can multiply terms in any order.
$$6 \times m \times n = m \times n \times 6$$

The Associative Property of Multiplication is shown here, which states that any group of numbers and/or variables can be grouped together in parentheses to be multiplied first before multiplying by the remaining numbers and/or variables.

$$4 \times (5a) = (4a) \times 5$$

The Identity Property of Addition is shown here, which states that adding 0 to any number or term does not change the value of that number or term.

$$s + 0 = s$$

The Associative Property of Addition is shown here, which states that any group of numbers and/or variables can be grouped together in parentheses to be added first before adding the remaining numbers and/or variables.

$$10 + (6 + 1) = (10 + 6) + 1$$

Coefficients and the Distributive Property

Coefficients
A coefficient is a number or symbol that is multiplied by a variable. For example, in the expression 2(ab), the number 2 is the coefficient of (ab). The expression can be written in other ways to have a different coefficient. For example, the expression can be 2a(b). This means that 2a is the coefficient of (b).

Distributive Property
The distributive property can be used to multiply each addend in parentheses. Then, the products are added to reach the result. The formula for the distributive property looks like this:

$$a(b + c) = ab + ac$$

Example: 6(2+4)
First, multiply 6 and 2. The answer is 12.
Then, multiply 6 and 4. The answer is 24.
Last, we add 12 and 24. So, the final answer is 36.

Rounding and Estimation

Rounding

Rounding is lowering the digits in a number and keeping the value similar. The result will be less accurate. However, this will be in a simpler form and will be easier to use. Whole numbers can be rounded to the nearest ten, hundred or thousand. Also, fractions and decimals can be rounded to the nearest whole number.

Example 1
Round each number to the nearest ten: 11 | 47 | 118

When rounding to the nearest ten, anything ending in 5 or greater rounds up.
So, 11 rounds to 10 | 47 rounds to 50 | 118 rounds to 120.

Example 2
Round each number to the nearest hundred: 78 | 980 | 248

When rounding to the nearest hundred, anything ending in 50 or greater rounds up.
So, 78 rounds to 100 | 980 rounds to 1000 | 248 rounds down to 200.

Example 3
Round each number to the nearest thousand: 302 | 1274 | 3756

When rounding to the nearest thousand, anything ending in 500 or greater rounds up.
So, 302 rounds to 0 | 1274 rounds to 1000 | 3756 rounds to 4000.

Example 4
Round each number to the nearest whole number: $\frac{5}{8}$ | 2.12 | $\frac{14}{3}$

When rounding fractions and decimals, anything half or higher rounds up.
So, $\frac{5}{8}$ rounds to 1 | 2.12 rounds to 2 | $\frac{14}{3}$ rounds to 5.

Estimation

Estimation is the process of finding an approximate answer to a problem. Estimation may involve rounding to the nearest whole number to make addition or subtraction easier.

Example 1
There are 24 people in an English class. Miss Foster decides to order three exam books for each student, plus 6 extras. She estimates that she should order 90 exam books. Identify if her solution is reasonable.

Write an expression to determine the total number of exam books to order. Since three books are ordered for each student, first multiply the number of books per student by the number of students: 3 books per student · 24 students = 72 books. Next, add the six extra exam books that Miss Foster would like to order. The total number of books to order is: 72 + 6 = 78 books. Her original estimate of 90 exam books is too large.

Example 2
The following food items are available in a school cafeteria for lunch:
Sandwich: $3.15; Soup: $1.84
Salad: $2.62; Pretzels: $0.95
Milk: $0.40

Daniel has $4.00 and wants to purchase a milk, sandwich, and soup. Emily has $4.00 and wants to purchase a salad, pretzels, and milk. Estimate the cost of each student's lunch and determine if they have enough money to purchase the food they would like for lunch.

Daniel wants to purchase a milk, sandwich, and soup. Rounded to the nearest fifty cents, the cost of his items is $0.50, $3.00, and $2.00. The total for his three items would be approximately:
$$0.50 + 3.00 + 2.00 = 5.50$$
It will cost Daniel approximately $5.50 for his lunch. He does not have enough money to purchase the items he has selected.

Emily wants to purchase a salad, pretzels, and milk. Rounded to the nearest fifty cents, the cost of her items is $2.50, $1.00, and $0.50. The total for her three items would be approximately:
$$2.50 + 1.00 + 0.50 = 4.00$$

It will cost Emily approximately $4.00 for her lunch. She has approximately enough money to purchase the items she has selected.

Decimals, Fractions, and Percents

Decimals

Decimal Illustration
Use a model to represent the decimal: 0.24. Write 0.24 as a fraction. The decimal 0.24 is twenty four hundredths. One possible model to represent this fraction is to draw 100 pennies, since each penny is worth 1 one hundredth of a dollar. Draw one hundred circles to represent one hundred pennies. Shade 24 of the pennies to represent the decimal twenty four hundredths.

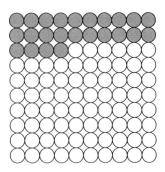

To write the decimal as a fraction, write a fraction: $\frac{\#\ shaded\ spaces}{\#\ total\ spaces}$. The number of shaded spaces is 24, and the total number of spaces is 100, so as a fraction 0.24 equals $\frac{24}{100}$. $\frac{24}{100}$ can then be reduced to $\frac{6}{25}$.

Adding and Subtracting Decimals
When adding and subtracting decimals, the decimal points must always be aligned. Adding decimals is just like adding regular whole numbers.
Example: 4.5 + 2 = 6.5.

If the problem-solver does not properly align the decimal points, an incorrect answer of 4.7 may result. An easy way to add decimals is to align all of the decimal points in a vertical column visually. This will allow one to see exactly where the decimal should be placed in the final answer. Begin adding from right to left. Add each column in turn, making sure to carry the number to the left if a column adds up to more than 9. The same rules apply to the subtraction of decimals.

> ➤ **Review Video:** <u>Adding and Subtracting Decimals</u>
> *Visit **mometrix.com/academy** and enter **Code: 381101***

Fractions

A fraction has one integer that is written above another integer with a dividing line between them $(\frac{x}{y})$. It represents the quotient of the two numbers "x divided by y." Also, this can be thought of as x out of y equal parts. The x and y in this fraction are known as variables. When the value for a symbol can change, a variable is given to that value. So, a number like 3 is a constant. A value that does not change is a constant.

The top number of a fraction is called the numerator. This number stands for the number of parts. The 1 in $\frac{1}{4}$ means that this is one part out of the whole. The bottom number of a fraction is called the denominator. This stands for the total number of equal parts. The 4 in $\frac{1}{4}$ means that the whole has four equal parts. A fraction cannot have a denominator of zero. This fraction is known as "undefined." The reverse of a fraction is known as the reciprocal. For example, the reciprocal of 1/2 is 2, and the reciprocal of 3 is 1/3.

Fractions can be changed by multiplying or dividing the numerator and denominator by the same number. This will not change the value of the fraction. You cannot do this with addition or subtraction. If you divide both numbers by a common factor, you will reduce or simplify the fraction. Two fractions that have the same value but are given in different ways are known as equivalent fractions. For example, $\frac{2}{10}, \frac{3}{15}, \frac{4}{20}$, and $\frac{5}{25}$ are equivalent fractions. Also, they can be reduced or simplified to $\frac{1}{5}$.

Two fractions can be changed to have the same denominator. This is known as finding a common denominator. The number for the common denominator should be the least common multiple of the original denominators. Example: $\frac{3}{4}$ and $\frac{5}{6}$; the least common multiple of 4 and 6 is 12. So, you can change these fractions to have a common denominator: $\frac{3}{4} = \frac{9}{12}$ and $\frac{5}{6} = \frac{10}{12}$.

If two fractions have a common denominator, you can add or subtract the fractions with the two numerators. Example: $\frac{1}{2} + \frac{1}{4} = \frac{2}{4} + \frac{1}{4} = \frac{3}{4}$. If the two fractions do not have the same denominator, one or both of them must be changed to have a common denominator. This needs to be done before they can be added or subtracted.

A fraction with a denominator that is greater than the numerator is known as a proper fraction. A fraction with a numerator that is greater than the denominator is known as an improper fraction. Proper fractions have values less than one. Improper fractions have values greater than one.

A mixed number is a number that has an integer and a fraction. Any improper fraction can be rewritten as a mixed number. Example: $\frac{8}{3} = \frac{6}{3} + \frac{2}{3} = 2 + \frac{2}{3} = 2\frac{2}{3}$.
Also, any mixed number can be rewritten as an improper fraction. Example: $1\frac{3}{5} = 1 + \frac{3}{5} = \frac{5}{5} + \frac{3}{5} = \frac{8}{5}$.

> **Review Video: <u>Fractions</u>**
*Visit **mometrix.com/academy** and enter **Code: 262335***

Converting Decimals to Fractions

A fraction can be turned into a decimal and vice versa. In order to convert a fraction into a decimal, simply divide the numerator by the denominator. For example, the fraction $\frac{5}{4}$ becomes 1.25. This is done by dividing 5 by 4. The fraction $\frac{4}{8}$ becomes 0.5 when 4 is divided by 8. This remains true even if the fraction $\frac{4}{8}$ is first reduced to $\frac{1}{2}$. The decimal conversion will still be 0.5. In order to convert a decimal into a fraction, count the number of places to the right of the decimal. This will be the number of zeros in the denominator. The numbers to the right of the decimal will become the whole number in the numerator.

Example 1:

$0.45 = \frac{45}{100}$

$\frac{45}{100}$ reduces to $\frac{9}{20}$

Example 2:

$0.237 = \frac{237}{1000}$

Example 3:

$0.2121 = \frac{2121}{10000}$

> **Review Video: <u>Converting Decimals to Fractions and Percentages</u>**
> *Visit **mometrix.com/academy** and enter **Code: 986765***

Percentages

You can think of percentages as fractions that are based on a whole of 100. In other words, one whole is equal to 100%. The word percent means "per hundred." Fractions can be given as percents by using equivalent fractions with an amount of 100. Example: $\frac{7}{10} = \frac{70}{100} = 70\%$; Another example is $\frac{1}{4} = \frac{25}{100} = 25\%$. To give a percentage as a fraction, divide the percentage by 100. Then, reduce the fraction to its simplest possible terms. Example: $60\% = \frac{60}{100} = \frac{3}{5}$; $96\% = \frac{96}{100} = \frac{24}{25}$.

Converting decimals to percentages and percentages to decimals is as simple as moving the decimal point. To convert from a decimal to a percent, move the decimal point two places to the right. To convert from a percent to a decimal, move the decimal two places to the left.
Example: 0.23 = 23%; 5.34 = 534%; 0.007 = 0.7%; 700% = 7.00; 86% = 0.86; 0.15% = 0.0015.

Ratios, Proportions, and Scale Drawings

Ratios
A ratio is a comparison of two numbers in a certain order. Example: There are 14 computers in a lab, and the class has 20 students. So, there is a student to computer ratio of 20 to 14. Normally, this is written as 20:14.

Ratios can be listed as *a to b*, *a:b*, or *a/b*. Examples of ratios are miles per hour (miles/hour), meters per second (meters/second), and miles per gallon (miles/gallon).

> **Review Video: <u>Ratios</u>**
> *Visit **mometrix.com/academy** and enter **Code: 996914***

<u>Proportions and Cross Products</u>
A proportion is a relationship between two numbers. This relationship shows how one changes when the other changes. A direct proportion is a relationship where a number increases by a set amount with every increase in the other number.

Another way is for the number to decrease by that same amount for every decrease in the other quantity. Example: For every 1 sheet cake, 18 people can have cake. The number of sheet cakes and the number of people that can be served from them is a direct proportion.

Inverse proportion is a relationship where an increase in one number has a decrease in the other. This can work the other way where a decrease in a number has an increase in the other. Example: The time needed for a car trip decreases as the speed increases. Also, the time for the trip increases as the speed decreases. So, the time needed for the trip is inversely proportional to the speed of the car.

Two equal ratios have cross products that are equal. This can be written as $\frac{m}{b} = \frac{w}{z}$. For example, Fred travels 2 miles in 1 hour, and Jane travels 4 miles in 2 hours. So, their speeds are proportional because $\frac{2}{1} = \frac{4}{2}$.

In a proportion, the product of the numerator of the first ratio and the denominator of the second ratio is equal to the product of the denominator of the first ratio and the numerator of the second ratio. In other words, you can see that $m \times z = b \times w$. So, $2 \times 2 = 1 \times 4$.

> ➤ **Review Video:** <u>Proportions</u>
> Visit *mometrix.com/academy* and enter *Code:* **505355**

<u>Actual Drawings and Scale Drawings</u>
A map has a key for measurements to compare real distances with a scale distance.
Example: The key on one map says that 2 inches on the map is 12 real miles. Find the distance of a route that is 5 inches long on the map.

A proportion is needed to show the map measurements and real distances. First, write a ratio that has the information in the key. The map measurement can be in the numerator, and the real distance can be in the denominator.

$$\frac{2 \text{ inches}}{12 \text{ miles}}$$

Next, write a ratio with the known map distance and the unknown real distance. The unknown number for miles can be represented with the letter m.

$$\frac{5 \text{ inches}}{m \text{ miles}}$$

Then, write out the ratios in a proportion and solve it for m.

$$\frac{2 \text{ inches}}{12 \text{ miles}} = \frac{5 \text{ inches}}{m \text{ miles}}$$

Now, you have $2m = 60$. So, you are left with $m = 30$. Thus, the route is 30 miles long.

Algebra, Functions, and Patterns

Translating

Words to Mathematical Expression

Write "four less than twice x" as a mathematical expression.

Remember that an expression does not have an equals sign. "Less" indicates subtraction, and "twice" indicates multiplication by two. Four less than $2x$ is $2x - 4$. Notice how this is different than $4 - 2x$. You can plug in values for x to see how these expressions would yield different values.

Words to Mathematical Equation

Translate "three hundred twenty-five increased by six times $3x$ equals three hundred forty-three" into a mathematical equation.

The key words and phrases are "increased by," "times," and "equals."
Three hundred twenty-five increased by six times $3x$ equals three hundred forty-three:
$$325 + 6(3x) = 343$$

The mathematical sentence is $325 + 6(3x) = 343$.

Mathematical Expression to a Phrase

Write a phrase which represents this mathematical expression: $75 - 3t + 14^2$.

Because there are many words which indicate various operations, there are several ways to write this expression, including "seventy-five minus three times t plus fourteen squared."

Solving for a Variable

Similar to order of operation rules, algebraic rules must be obeyed to ensure a correct answer. Begin by locating all parentheses and brackets, and then solving the equations within them. Then, perform the operations necessary to remove all parentheses and brackets. Next, convert all fractions into whole numbers and combine common terms on each side of the equation.

Beginning on the left side of the expression, solve operations involving multiplication and division. Then, work left to right solving operations involving addition and subtraction. Finally, cross-multiply if necessary to reach the final solution.

Example 1
$4a-10=10$

Constants are the numbers in equations that do not change. The variable in this equation is a. Variables are most commonly presented as either x or y, but they can be any letter. Every variable is equal to a number; one must solve the equation to determine what that number is. In an algebraic expression, the answer will usually be the number represented by the variable. In order to solve this equation, keep in mind that what is done to one side must be done to the other side as well. The first step will be to remove 10 from the left side by adding 10 to both sides. This will be expressed as $4a-10+10=10+10$, which simplifies to $4a=20$. Next, remove the 4 by dividing both sides by 4. This step will be expressed as $4a\div4=20\div4$. The expression now becomes $a=5$.

Since variables are the letters that represent an unknown number, you must solve for that unknown number in single variable problems. The main thing to remember is that you can do anything to one side of an equation as long as you do it to the other.

<u>Example 2</u>
Solve for x in the equation 2x + 3 = 5.

Answer: First you want to get the "2x" isolated by itself on one side. To do that, first get rid of the 3. Subtract 3 from both sides of the equation 2x + 3 – 3 = 5 – 3 or 2x = 2. Now since the x is being multiplied by the 2 in "2x", you must divide by 2 to get rid of it. So, divide both sides by 2, which gives 2x / 2 = 2 / 2 or x = 1.

Manipulating Equations

Sometimes you will have variables missing in equations. So, you need to find the missing variable. To do this, you need to remember one important thing: whatever you do to one side of an equation, you need to do to the other side. If you subtract 100 from one side of an equation, you need to subtract 100 from the other side of the equation. This will allow you to change the form of the equation to find missing values.

<u>Example</u>
Ray earns $10 an hour. This can be given with the expression $10x$, where x is equal to the number of hours that Ray works. This is the independent variable. The independent variable is the amount that can change. The money that Ray earns is in y hours. So, you would write the equation: $10x = y$. The variable y is the dependent variable. This depends on x and cannot be changed. Now, let's say that Ray makes $360. How many hours did he work to make $360?
$$10x = 360$$

Now, you want to know how many hours that Ray worked. So, you want to get x by itself. To do that, you can divide both sides of the equation by 10.
$$\frac{10x}{10} = \frac{360}{10}$$

So, you have: $x = 36$. Now, you know that Ray worked 36 hours to make $360.

Functions

<u>Example 1</u>
The table below is the value of each part of an ordered pair. An ordered pair is written as: (x, y)

x	y
2	6
4	12
6	18
8	24

You can find y if you know x. The number in the y column is three times the number in the x column. Multiply the x number by 3 to get the y number.

x	y
2	$2 \times 3 = 6$
4	$4 \times 3 = 12$
6	$6 \times 3 = 18$
8	$8 \times 3 = 24$

Example 2
The table shows some data points for a linear function. What is the missing value in the table?

x	y
0	?
3	50
5	80

The data in the table represent a linear function. For a linear function, the rate of change is equal to the slope. To find the slope, calculate the change in y divided by the change in x for the two given points from the table: $m = \frac{80-50}{5-3} = \frac{30}{2} = 15$

The rate of change of the linear function is 15. This means for each increase of 1 in the value of x, the value of y increases by 15. Similarly, each decrease of 1 in the value of x decreases the value of y by 15. The x-value 0 is 3 less than 3, so subtract $3 \cdot 15 = 45$ from 50 to get y = 5. This is the missing value in the table.

Sequencing

Example 1
Use the sequence to find each of the following.
6, 13, 20, 27, 34, 41, ...
a) Find the position of 34.

b) Find the value of the term in position 7.

a) The position of a term is its place in the sequence. The sequence begins with 6, in position 1, 13 is position 2, etc. The term 34 has a position of 5.

b) The terms in positions 1 through 6 are given. To find the term in position 7, identify the difference between each term.
13 – 6 = 7
20 – 13 = 7
27 – 20 = 7
34 – 27 = 7
41 – 34 = 7

The terms are increasing by 7. To find the 7th term, add 7 to the sixth term, 41:
41 + 7 = 48
The term in position 7 is 48.

<u>Example 2</u>
The nth term of a sequence is: $4n - 6$. Find the terms in position: 1, 4, and 10.

To find the terms in each given position, evaluate the expression for the nth term at the given position values.
1st term: $4(1) - 6 = 4 - 6 = -2$
4th term: $4(4) - 6 = 16 - 6 = 10$
10th term: $4(10) - 6 = 40 - 6 = 34$

<u>Example 3</u>
Write an algebraic expression to determine the nth term of the arithmetic sequence:
31, 25, 19, 13, ...

To find the nth term, find the common difference between each pair of given terms.
2nd term – 1st term: $25 - 31 = -6$
3rd term – 2nd term: $19 - 25 = -6$
4th term – 3rd term: $13 - 19 = -6$
The first term is 31, so when $n = 1$, the term is 31.
1st term: $31 + -6(n - 1)$

Simplify this expression and check it for terms 2, 3, and 4 by evaluating the expression at $n = 2, 3,$ and 4.
$31 + -6(n - 1) = 31 - 6n + 6 = -6n + 37$
2nd term: $-6(2) + 37 = -12 + 37 = 25$
3rd term: $-6(3) + 37 = -18 + 37 = 19$
4th term: $-6(4) + 37 = -24 + 37 = 13$
The nth term of the arithmetic sequence is $-6n + 37$.

Geometry

Lines and Planes

A point is a fixed location in space. This point has no size or dimensions. Commonly, this fixed location is a dot. A collinear point is a point which is on the line. A non-collinear point is a point that is not on a line.

A line is a set of points that go forever in two opposite directions. The line has length but no width or depth. A line can be named by any two points that are on the line. A line segment is a part of a line that has definite endpoints. A ray is a part of a line that goes from a single point and goes in one direction along the line. A ray has a definite beginning but no ending.

A plane is a two-dimensional flat surface that has three non-collinear points. A plane goes an unending distance in all directions in those two dimensions. This plane has an unending number of points, parallel lines and segments, intersecting lines and segments. Also, a plane can have an unending number of parallel or intersecting rays. A plane will never have a three-dimensional figure or skew lines. Two given planes will be parallel, or they will intersect to form a line. A plane may intersect a circular conic surface (e.g., a cone) to make conic sections (e.g., the parabola, hyperbola, circle, or ellipse).

Perpendicular lines are lines that intersect at right angles. The symbol ⊥ stands for perpendicular lines. The shortest distance from a line to a point that is not on the line is a perpendicular segment from the point to the line.

Parallel lines are lines in the same plane that have no points in common and never meet. The lines can be in different planes, have no points in common, and never meet. However, the lines will not be parallel because they are in different planes.

A bisector is a line or line segment that divides another line segment into two equal lengths. A perpendicular bisector of a line segment has points that are equidistant (i.e., equal distances) from the endpoints of the segment.

Intersecting lines are lines that have exactly one point in common. Concurrent lines are several lines that intersect at a single point. A transversal is a line that intersects at least two other lines. The lines may or may not be parallel to one another. A transversal that intersects parallel lines is common in geometry.

Coordinate Plane

Often, algebraic functions and equations are shown on a graph. This graph is known as the *Cartesian Coordinate Plane*. The Cartesian coordinate plane has two number lines that are perpendicular. These lines intersect at the zero point. This point is also known as the origin. The horizontal number line is known as the x-axis.

On the x-axis, there are positive values to the right of the origin and negative values to the left of the origin. The vertical number line is known as the y-axis. There are positive values above the origin and negative values below the origin. Any point on the plane can be found with an ordered pair.

This ordered pair comes in the form of (x, y). This pair is known as coordinates. The x-value of the coordinate is called the abscissa. The y-value of the coordinate is called the ordinate. The two number lines divide the plane into four parts. Each part is known as a quadrant. The quadrants are labeled as I, II, III, and IV.

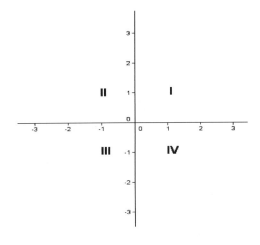

<u>Example 1</u>
The following points go on the coordinate plane:
A. (−4, −2) | B. (−1, 3) | C. (2, 2) | D. (3, −1)

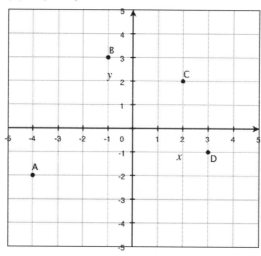

Transformation

- Rotation: An object is rotated, or turned, between 0 and 360 degrees, around a fixed point. The size and shape of the object are unchanged.
- Reflection: An object is reflected, or flipped, across a line, so that the original object and reflected object are the same distance from the line of reflection. The size and shape of the object are unchanged.
- Translation: An object is translated, or shifted, horizontally and/or vertically to a new location. The orientation, size, and shape of the object are unchanged.

<u>Rotation</u>
A line segment begins at (1, 4) and ends at (5, 4). Draw the line segment and rotate the line segment 90º about the point (3, 4).
The point about which the line segment is being rotated is on the line segment. This point should be on both the original and rotated line. The point (3, 4) is the center of the original line segment, and should still be the center of the rotated line segment. The dashed line is the rotated line segment.

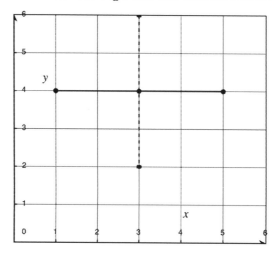

- 20 -

Reflection

Example 1: To create a congruent rectangle by reflecting, first draw a line of reflection. The line can be next to or on the figure. Then draw the image reflected across this line.

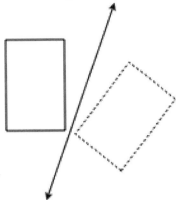

Example 2: A line segment begins at (1, 5) and ends at (5, 4). Draw the line segment, then reflect the line segment across the line $y = 3$.

To reflect a segment, consider folding a piece of paper at the line of reflection. The new image should line up exactly with the old image when the paper is folded. The dashed line is the reflected line segment.

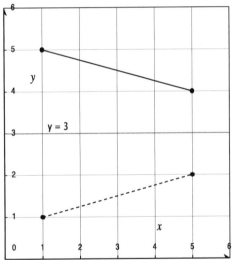

Translation

Example 1: A line segment on an x-y grid starts at (3, 2) and ends at (4, 1). Draw the line segment, and translate the segment up 2 units and left 2 units.

The solid line segment is the original line segment, and the dashed line is the translated line segment. The *y*-coordinate of each point has increased by 2, because the points moved two units away from 0. The *x*-coordinate of each point has decreased by 2, because the points moved two units closer to 0.

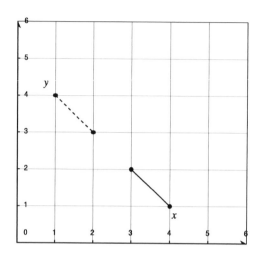

Example 2: Identify a transformation that could have been performed on the solid triangle to result in the dashed triangle.

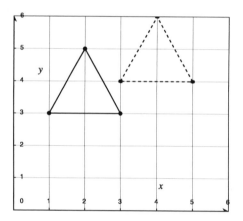

The transformed triangle has the same orientation as the original triangle. It has been shifted up one unit and two units to the right. Because the orientation of the figure has not changed, and its new position can be described using shifts up and to the right, the figure was translated.

Angles

An angle is made when two lines or line segments meet at a point. The angle may be a starting point for a pair of segments or rays. Also, angles come from the intersection of lines. The symbol $\angle$ stands for angles. Angles that are opposite to one another are called vertical angles, and their measures are equal. The vertex is the point where two segments or rays meet to make an angle. Angles that are made from intersecting rays, lines, and/or line segments have four angles at the vertex.

An acute angle is an angle with a degree measure less than 90°. A right angle is an angle with a degree measure of exactly 90°. An obtuse angle is an angle with a degree measure greater than 90° but less than 180°. A straight angle is an angle with a degree measure of exactly 180°. A reflex angle is an angle with a degree measure greater than 180° but less than 360°. A full angle is an angle with a degree measure of exactly 360°.

> **Review Video: Angles**
> *Visit **mometrix.com/academy** and enter **Code: 264624***

Two angles with a sum of exactly 90° are known as complementary. The two angles may or may not be adjacent (i.e., *next to* or *beside*). In a right triangle, the two acute angles are complementary.

Two angles with a sum that is exactly 180° are known as supplementary. The two angles may or may not be adjacent. Two intersecting lines always make two pairs of supplementary angles. Adjacent supplementary angles will always make a straight line.

Triangles

An equilateral triangle is a triangle with three congruent sides. Also, an equilateral triangle will have three congruent angles and each angle will be 60°. All equilateral triangles are acute triangles.

An isosceles triangle is a triangle with two congruent sides. An isosceles triangle will have two congruent angles as well.

A scalene triangle is a triangle with no congruent sides. Also, a scalene triangle will have three angles of different measures. The angle with the largest measure is opposite from the longest side. The angle with the smallest measure is opposite from the shortest side.

An acute triangle is a triangle whose three angles are all less than 90°. If two of the angles are equal, the acute triangle is also an isosceles triangle. If the three angles are all equal, the acute triangle is also an equilateral triangle.

A right triangle is a triangle with exactly one angle equal to 90°. A right triangle can never be acute or obtuse.

An obtuse triangle is a triangle with one angle greater than 90°. The other two angles may or may not be equal. If the two remaining angles are equal, the obtuse triangle is also an isosceles triangle.

Congruency, Similarity, and Symmetry

Congruent figures are geometric figures that have the same size and shape. All corresponding angles are equal, and all corresponding sides are equal. Congruence is shown by the symbol ≅.

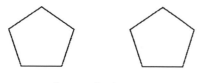

Congruent polygons

Similar figures are geometric figures that have the same shape, but may not have the same size. All corresponding angles are equal, and all corresponding sides are proportional. However, they do not have to be equal. Similarity is shown by the symbol ∿.

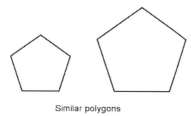

Similar polygons

Note that all congruent figures are also similar. However, not all similar figures are congruent.

Line of Symmetry: The line that divides a figure or object into equal parts. Each part is congruent to the other. An object may have no lines of symmetry, one line of symmetry, or multiple (i.e., more than one) lines of symmetry.

Lines of symmetry:

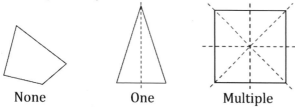

None   One   Multiple

Polygons and Two-Dimensional Figures

Each straight line segment of a polygon is called a side. The point at which two sides of a polygon intersect is called the vertex. In a polygon, the number of sides is always equal to the number of vertices. A polygon with all sides congruent and all angles equal is called a regular polygon.

A line segment from the center of a polygon that is perpendicular to a side of the polygon is called the apothem. A line segment from the center of a polygon to a vertex of the polygon is called a radius. In a regular polygon, the apothem can be used to find the area of the polygon using the formula $A = \frac{1}{2}ap$, where a is the apothem, and p is the perimeter.

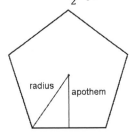

Triangle – 3 sides
Quadrilateral – 4 sides
Pentagon – 5 sides
Hexagon – 6 sides
Heptagon – 7 sides
Octagon – 8 sides
Nonagon – 9 sides
Decagon – 10 sides
Dodecagon – 12 sides

Generally, an *n*-gon is a polygon that has more than 12 angles and sides. The space of *n* is for the number of sides. Also, an 11-sided polygon is known as an 11-gon.

Quadrilateral: A closed two-dimensional geometric figure that has four straight sides. The sum of the interior angles of any quadrilateral is 360°. A quadrilateral whose diagonals divide each other is a parallelogram.

A quadrilateral whose opposite sides are parallel (i.e., 2 pairs of parallel sides) is a parallelogram. A quadrilateral whose diagonals are perpendicular bisectors of each other is a rhombus. A quadrilateral with opposite sides (i.e., both pairs) that are parallel and congruent is a rhombus.

Parallelogram: A quadrilateral that has two pairs of opposite parallel sides. The sides that are parallel are also congruent. The opposite interior angles are always congruent, and the consecutive interior angles are supplementary. The diagonals of a parallelogram divide each other. Each diagonal divides the parallelogram into two congruent triangles.

A parallelogram that has a right angle is a rectangle. In the diagram below, the top left corner and the bottom left corner are consecutive angles. Consecutive angles of a parallelogram are supplementary. If there is one right angle in a parallelogram, there are four right angles in that parallelogram.

Trapezoid: Normally, a quadrilateral has one pair of parallel sides. Some define a trapezoid as a quadrilateral that has at least one pair of parallel sides. There are no rules for the second pair of sides. So, there are no rules for the diagonals of a trapezoid.

Rectangles, rhombuses, and squares are all special forms of parallelograms.

Rectangle: A parallelogram with four right angles. All rectangles are parallelograms, but not all parallelograms are rectangles. The diagonals of a rectangle are congruent.

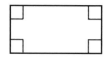

Rhombus: A parallelogram with four congruent sides. All rhombuses are parallelograms, but not all parallelograms are rhombuses. The diagonals of a rhombus are perpendicular to each other.

A rhombus with one right angle is a square. The rhombus is a special form of a parallelogram. So, the rules about the angles of a parallelogram are true for the rhombus.

Square: A parallelogram with four right angles and four congruent sides. All squares are also parallelograms, rhombuses, and rectangles. The diagonals of a square are congruent and perpendicular to each other.

Three Dimensional Figures

Right Rectangular Prism
A rectangular prism has six rectangular faces. The six faces give it 12 edges and eight vertices.

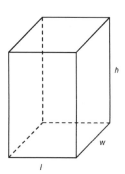

Cube
A cube has six square faces. The six faces give it 12 edges and eight vertices.

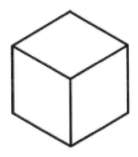

Sphere
A sphere is a perfectly round object that has no faces, edges, or vertices. This three-dimensional object is similar to the two-dimensional circle.

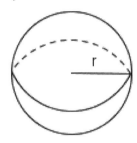

Right Triangular Prism
A triangular prism has five faces. Two faces are triangles, and three faces are rectangles. This prism has 9 edges and six vertices.

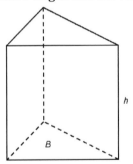

Cylinder
The cylinder has two circular faces. In three dimensions, the cylinder has edges or vertices.

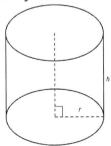

A rectangular pyramid has four triangular faces and one rectangular face. This pyramid has eight edges and five vertices.

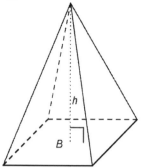

Cone

A cone has one circular face. Cones do not have any edges or vertices. The cones that you will encounter are right circular. This means that they have a circle for a base instead of a polygonal base. A pyramid is a cone with a polygonal base.

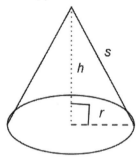

Measurement

Area and Perimeter Formulas

The perimeter of any triangle is found by adding the three side lengths $P = a + b + c$. For an equilateral triangle, this is the same as $P = 3s$, where s is any side length. The reason is that the three sides are the same length.

The area of any triangle can be found by taking half of the base (i.e., b). Then, multiply that result by the height (i.e., h) of the triangle. So, the standard formula for the area of a triangle is $A = \frac{1}{2}bh$. For many triangles, it may be difficult to calculate h. So, other formulas are given here that may be easier.

Note: When you need to find the height, you can follow the steps above to find it.

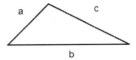

➤ **Review Video:** Area and Perimeter of a Triangle
*Visit **mometrix.com/academy** and enter **Code: 853779***

Another formula that works for any triangle is $A = \sqrt{s(s-a)(s-b)(s-c)}$, where A is the area, s is the semi-perimeter $s = \frac{a+b+c}{2}$, and a, b, and c are the lengths of the three sides. The area of an equilateral triangle can be found by the formula $A = \frac{\sqrt{3}}{4}s^2$, where A is the area and s is the length of a side. You could use the $30° - 60° - 90°$ ratios to find the height of the triangle. Then, use the standard triangle area formula.

The area of an isosceles triangle can be found by the formula, $A = \frac{1}{2}b\sqrt{a^2 - \frac{b^2}{4}}$, where A is the area, b is the base, and a is the length of one of the two congruent sides. If you do not remember this formula, you can use the Pythagorean Theorem to find the height. Then, you can use the standard formula for the area of a triangle.

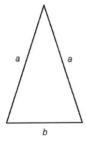

The area of a square is found by using the formula $A = s^2$, where A is the area and s is the length of one side.

The perimeter of a square is found by using the formula $P = 4s$, where P is the perimeter, and s is the length of one side. All four sides are equal in a square. So, you can multiply the length of one side by 4. This is faster than adding the same number four times.

➤ **Review Video:** Area and Perimeter of a Square
*Visit **mometrix.com/academy** and enter **Code: 620902***

The area of a rectangle is found by the formula $A = lw$, where A is the area of the rectangle, l is the length and w is the width. Usually, the longer side is the length, and the shorter side is the width. However, the numbers for l and w can used be for one or the other.

The perimeter of a rectangle can be found with two formulas $P = 2l + 2w$ or $P = 2(l + w)$, where l is the length, and w is the width.

➤ **Review Video:** Area and Perimeter of a Rectangle
*Visit **mometrix.com/academy** and enter **Code: 933707***

The area of a parallelogram is found by the formula $A = bh$, where b is the length of the base, and h is the height. Note that the base and height match with the length and width in a rectangle. So, this formula can be used for rectangles as well. Do not confuse the height of a parallelogram with the length of the second side. They have the same measure only with rectangles.

The perimeter of a parallelogram is found by the formula $P = 2a + 2b$ or $P = 2(a + b)$, where a and b are the lengths of the two sides.

> ➢ **Review Video:** <u>Area and Perimeter of a Parallelogram</u>
> *Visit **mometrix.com/academy** and enter **Code: 718313***

The area of a trapezoid is found by the formula $A = \frac{1}{2}h(b_1 + b_2)$, where h is the height, and b_1 and b_2 are the two parallel sides (i.e., bases). The height is the segment that joins the parallel bases.

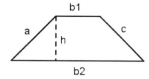

The perimeter of a trapezoid is found by the formula $P = a + b_1 + c + b_2$, where a, b_1, c, and b_2 are the four sides of the trapezoid.

> ➢ **Review Video:** <u>Area and Perimeter of a Trapezoid</u>
> *Visit **mometrix.com/academy** and enter **Code: 587523***

Circles

The center is the single point inside the circle that is equidistant from every point on the circle. The point O is in the diagram below. The radius is a line segment that joins the center of the circle and any one point on the circle. All radii of a circle are equal. The segments OX, OY, and OZ are in the diagram below. The diameter is a line segment that passes through the center of the circle and has both endpoints inside the circle. The length of the diameter is twice the length of the radius. The segment XZ is in the diagram below. Concentric circles are circles that have the same center but not the same length of radii. A bulls-eye target is an example of concentric circles.

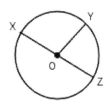

The **area of a circle** is found with the formula $A = \pi r^2$, where r is the length of the radius. If the diameter of the circle is given, divide it in half to get the radius before using the formula. (Note: In the following formulas, 3.14 is used for π.)

The **circumference of a circle** is found by the formula $C = 2\pi r$, where r is the radius.

> ➢ **Review Video:** <u>Area and Circumference of a Circle</u>
> *Visit **mometrix.com/academy** and enter **Code: 243015***

Surface Area and Volume Formulas

Rectangular Prism

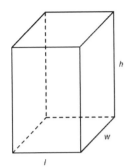

The **volume of a rectangular prism** can be found with the formula $V = lwh$, where V is the volume, l is the length, w is the width, and h is the height.

The **surface area of a rectangular prism** can be calculated as $SA = 2lw + 2hl + 2wh$ or $SA = 2(lw + hl + wh)$.

> ➤ **Review Video: Volume and Surface Area of a Rectangular Solid**
> *Visit* **mometrix.com/academy** *and enter* **Code: 386780**

Cube

The **volume of a cube** can be found with the formula $V = s^3$, where s is the length of a side.

The **surface area of a cube** is calculated as $SA = 6s^2$, where SA is the total surface area and s is the length of a side. These formulas are the same as the ones used for the volume and surface area of a rectangular prism. However, these are simple formulas because the three numbers (i.e., length, width, and height) are the same.

Temperature

Find the temperature, in degrees Fahrenheit, on the thermometer below. Use the thermometer to find the temperature if the temperature increased by 5° Fahrenheit.

The temperature, on the thermometer, is 75° F. If the temperature increases by 5° F, change the thermometer to show the increase in 5°:

If the temperature increases by 5° F, the new temperature is 80° F.

Time

Lindsay leaves for school at 7:00am. It takes her 20 minutes to get to school. Use a clock to determine the time Lindsay arrives at school. 7:00 am means the large clock hand is on 12, and the small hand is on 7.

In 20 minutes, the big hand will move 20 minutes clockwise, to the 4. The big hand will also move closer to the 8. 20 minutes is: $\frac{20}{60} = \frac{1}{3}$ of an hour, so the big hand will move one third of the way from the 7 to the 8.

The ending time is 7:20am, which is when Lindsay arrives at school.

Data Analysis and Probability

Measures of Central Tendency

The quantities of mean, median, and mode are known as measures of central tendency. Each can give a picture of what a whole set of data looks like with a single number. Knowing what each value stands for is important to understanding the information from these measures.

Mean
The mean, or the arithmetic mean or average, of a data set is found by adding all of the values in the set. Then you divide the sum by how many values that you had in a set. For example, a data set has 6 numbers, and the sum of those 6 numbers is 30. So, the mean is 30/6 = 5. When you know the

average, you may be asked to find a missing value. Look over the following steps for how this is done.

Example: You are given the values of 5, 10, 12, and 13. Also, you are told that the average is 9.6. So, what is the one missing value?

First: Add the known values together: $5 + 10 + 12 + 13 = 40$.
Now, set up an equation with the sum of the known values in the divisor. Then, put the number of values in the dividend.

For this example, you have 5 values. So, you have $\frac{40+?}{5} = 9.6$. Now, multiply both sides by 5:

$5 \times \frac{40+?}{5} = 9.6 \times 5$

Second: You are left with $40 + ? = 48$. Now, subtract 40 from both sides: $40 - 40 + ? = 48 - 40$. So, you know that the missing value is 8.

Median

The median is the middle value of a data set. The median can be found by putting the data set in numerical order (e.g., 3, 7, 26, 28, 39). Then, you pick the value that is in the middle of the set. In the data set (1, 2, 3, 4, 5), there is an odd number of values. So, the median is 3. Sometimes, there is an even number of values in the set. So, the median can be found by taking the average of the two middle values. In the data set (1, 2, 3, 4, 5, 6), the median would be $(3 + 4)/2 = 3.5$.

Mode

The mode is the value that appears the most in a data set. In the data set (1, 2, 3, 4, 5, 5, 5), the number 5 appears more than the other numbers. So, the value 5 is the mode. If more than one value appears the same number of times, then there are multiple values for the mode. For example, a data set is (1, 2, 2, 3, 4, 4, 5, 5). So, the modes would be 2, 4, and 5. Now, if no value appears more than any other value in the data set, then there is no mode.

> **Review Video:** <u>Mean, Median, and Mode</u>
> Visit **mometrix.com/academy** and enter **Code: 286207**

Range

The range is the difference between the greatest data point and the least data point in the set. In the set (12, 23, 1, 8, 45, 22), the greatest data point is 45. The least data point is 1. When you subtract 1 from 45, you have 44. So, 44 is the range of the data set.

Common Charts and Graphs

Charts and *Tables* are ways of organizing information into separate rows and columns. These rows and columns are labeled to find and to explain the information in them. Some charts and tables are organized horizontally with rows giving the details about the labeled information. Other charts and tables are organized vertically with columns giving the details about the labeled information.

A *Bar Graph* is one of the few graphs that can be drawn correctly in two ways: horizontally and vertically. A bar graph is similar to a line plot because of how the data is organized on the graph. Both axes must have their categories defined for the graph to be useful. A thick line is drawn from zero to the exact value of the data. This line can be used for a number, a percentage, or other numerical value. Longer bar lengths point to greater data values. To understand a bar graph, read the labels for the axes to know the units being reported. Then look where the bars end and match this to the scale on the other axis. This will show you the connection between the axes. This bar graph shows the responses from a survey about the favorite colors of a group.

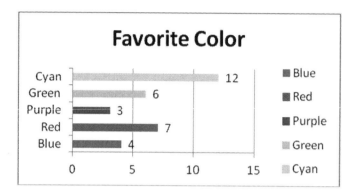

Line Graphs have one or more lines of different styles (e.g., solid or broken). These lines show the different values for a data set. Each point on the graph is shown as an ordered pair. This is similar to a Cartesian plane. In this case, the *x*- and *y*- axes are given certain units (e.g., dollars or time). Each point that is for one measurement is joined by line segments. Then, these lines show what the values are doing. The lines may be increasing (i.e., line sloping upward), decreasing (i.e., line sloping downward), or staying the same (i.e., horizontal line). More than one set of data can be put on the same line graph. This is done to compare more than one piece of data. An example of this would be graphing test scores for different groups of students over the same stretch of time. This allows you to see which group had the greatest increase or decrease in performance over a certain amount of years. This example is shown in the graph below.

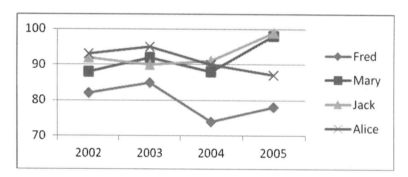

A *Line Plot*, or a *Dot Plot*, has plotted points that are NOT connected by line segments. In this graph, the horizontal axis lists the different possible values for the data. The vertical axis lists how many times one value happens. A single dot is graphed for each value. The dots in a line plot are connected. If the dots are connected, then this will not correctly represent the data.

A *Pictograph* is a graph that is given in the horizontal format. This graph uses pictures or symbols to show the data. Each pictograph must have a key that defines the picture or symbol. Also, this key should give the number that stands for each picture or symbol. The pictures or symbols on a pictograph are not always shown as whole elements.

In this case, the fraction of the picture or symbol stands for the same fraction of the quantity that a whole picture or symbol represents. For example, there is a row in the pictograph with $3\frac{1}{2}$ ears of corn. Each ear of corn represents 100 stalks of corn in a field. So, this would equal $3\frac{1}{2} \times 100 = 350$ stalks of corn in the field.

Circle Graphs, or *Pie Charts*, show the relationship of each type of data compared to the whole set of data. The circle graph is divided into sections by drawing radii (i.e., plural for radius) to make central angles. These angles stand for a percentage of the circle. Each 1% of data is equal to 3.6° in the graph. So, data that stands for a 90° section of the circle graph makes up 25% of the whole. The pie chart below shows the data from the frequency table where people were asked about their favorite color.

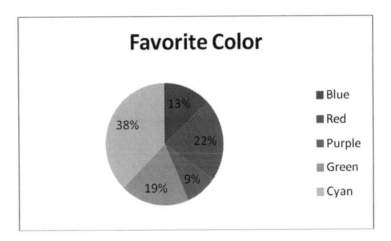

Probability

Probability is a branch of statistics that deals with the likelihood of something taking place. One classic example is a coin toss. There are only two possible results: heads or tails. The likelihood, or probability, that the coin will land as heads is 1 out of 2 (i.e., 1/2, 0.5, 50%). Tails has the same probability. Another common example is a 6-sided die roll. There are six possible results from rolling a single die. So, each side has an equal chance of happening. So, the probability of any number coming up is 1 out of 6.

> **Review Video:** <u>Simple Probability</u>
*Visit **mometrix.com/academy** and enter **Code: 212374***

Reading Comprehension

Reading and Thinking

Organization of the Passage

The way a passage is organized can help readers to understand the author's purpose and his or her conclusions. There are many ways to organize a passage, and each one has an important use.

Sometimes authors will organize information clearly for you to follow and locate the information. However, this is not always the case with passages in an exam. Two common ways to order a passage are cause and effect and chronological order. When using **chronological order** (i.e., a plan that moves in order from the first step to the last), the author gives information in the order that the event happened. For example, biographies are written in chronological order. The person's birth and childhood are first. Their adult life is next. The events leading up to the person's death are last.

Purposes for Writing

An **informative passage** is written to teach readers. Informative passages are almost always nonfiction. The purpose of an informative passage is to share information in the clearest way. In an informative passage, you may have a thesis statement (i.e., an argument on the topic of a passage that is explained by proof). A thesis statement is a sentence that normally comes at end of the first paragraph. Authors of informative passages are likely to put more importance on being clear. Informative passages do not normally appeal to the feelings. They often contain facts and figures. Informative passages almost never include the opinion of the author. However, you should know that there can be a bias in the facts. Sometimes, a persuasive passage can be like an informative passage. This is true when authors give their ideas as if they were facts.

Entertainment passages describe real or imagined people, places, and events. Entertainment passages are often stories or poems. So, figurative language is a common part of these passages. Often, an entertainment passage appeals to the imagination and feelings. Authors may persuade or inform in an entertainment passage. Or, an entertainment passage may cause readers to think differently about a subject.

When authors want to **share feelings,** they may use strong language. Authors may share feelings about a moment of great pain or happiness. Other times, authors will try to persuade readers by sharing feelings. Some phrases like *I felt* and *I sense* hint that the author is sharing feelings. Authors may share a story of deep pain or great joy. You must not be influenced by these stories. You need to keep some distance to judge the author's argument.

Almost all writing is descriptive. In one way or another, authors try to describe events, ideas, or people. Some texts are concerned only with **description**. A descriptive passage focuses on a single subject and seeks to explain the subject clearly. Descriptive passages contain many adjectives and adverbs (i.e., words that give a complete picture for you to imagine). Normally, a descriptive passage is informative. Yet, the passage may be persuasive or entertaining.

Writing Devices

Authors will use different writing devices to make their message clear for readers. One of those devices is comparison and contrast. When authors show how two things are alike, they are **comparing** them. When authors describe how two things are different, they are **contrasting** them. The compare and contrast passage is a common part of nonfiction. Comparisons are known by certain words or phrases: *both, same, like, too,* and *as well.* Yet, contrasts may have words or phrases like *but, however, on the other hand, instead,* and *yet.* Of course, comparisons and contrasts may be understood without using those words or phrases. A single sentence may compare and contrast. Think about the sentence *Brian and Sheila love ice cream, but Brian loves vanilla and Sheila loves strawberry.* In one sentence, the author has described both a similarity (e.g., love of ice cream) and a difference (e.g., favorite flavor).

> ➤ **Review Video:** <u>Compare and Contrast</u>
> *Visit **mometrix.com/academy** and enter **Code: 798319**

Point of view has an important influence on a passage. A passage's point of view is how the author or a character sees or thinks about things. A point of view influences the events of a passage, the meetings among characters, and the ending to the story. For example, two characters watch a child ride a bike. Character one watches outside. Character two watches from inside a house. Both see the same event, yet they are around different noises, sights, and smells. Character one may see different things that happen outside that character two cannot see from inside. Also, point of view can be influenced by past events and beliefs. For example, if character one loves bikes, then she will remember how proud she is of the child. If character two is afraid of riding bikes, then he may not remember the event or fear for the child's safety.

In fiction, the two main points of view are first person and third person. The narrator is the person who tells a story's events. The protagonist is the main character of a story. If the narrator is the protagonist in a story, then the story is written in first-person. In first person, the author writes from the view of *I.* Third-person point of view is the most common among stories. With third person, authors refer to each character by using *he* or *she* and the narrator is not involved in the story. In third-person omniscient, the narrator is not a character in the story and tells the story of all of the characters at the same time.

> ➤ **Review Video:** <u>Point of View</u>
> *Visit **mometrix.com/academy** and enter **Code: 383336**

Transitional words and phrases are devices that guide readers through a passage. You may know the common transitions. Though you may not have thought about how they are used. Some transitional phrases (*after, before, during, in the middle of*) give information about time. Some hint that an example is about to be given (*for example, in fact, for instance*). Writers use transitions to compare (*also, likewise*) and contrast (*however, but, yet*). Transitional words and phrases can point to addition (*and, also, furthermore, moreover*) and understood relationships (*if, then, therefore, as a result, since*). Finally, transitional words and phrases can separate the chronological steps (*first, second, last*).

> ➤ **Review Video:** <u>Transitional Words and Phrases</u>
> *Visit **mometrix.com/academy** and enter **Code: 197796**

Understanding a Passage

One of the most important skills in reading comprehension is finding **topics** and **main ideas.** There is a small difference between these two. The topic is the subject of a passage (i.e., what the passage is all about). The main idea is the most important argument being made by the author. The topic is shared in a few words while the main idea needs a full sentence to be understood. As an example, a short passage might have the topic of penguins, and the main idea could be written as *Penguins are different from other birds in many ways.*

In most nonfiction writing, the topic and the main idea will be stated clearly. Sometimes, they will come in a sentence at the very beginning or end of the passage. When you want to know the topic, you may find it in the first sentence of each paragraph. A body paragraph's first sentence is often-- but not always--the main topic sentence. The topic sentence gives you a summary of the ideas in the paragraph. You may find that the topic or main idea is not given clearly. So, you must read every sentence of the passage. Then, try to come up with an overall idea from each sentence.

Note: A thesis statement is not the same as the main idea. The main idea gives a brief, general summary of a text. The thesis statement gives a clear idea on an issue that is backed up with evidence.

> ➤ **Review Video:** <u>Topics and Main Ideas</u>
> *Visit mometrix.com/academy and enter Code:* **407801**

The main idea is the umbrella argument of a passage. So, **supporting details** back up the main idea. To show that a main idea is correct, authors add details that prove their idea. All passages contain details. However, they are supporting details when the details help an argument in the passage.

Supporting details are found in informative and persuasive texts. Sometimes they will come with terms like *for example* or *for instance.* Or, they will be numbered with terms like *first, second,* and *last.* You should think about how the author's supporting details back up his or her main idea. Supporting details can be correct, yet they may help the author's main idea. Sometimes supporting details can seem helpful. However, they may be useless when they are based on opinions.

> ➤ **Review Video:** <u>Supporting Details</u>
> *Visit mometrix.com/academy and enter Code:* **396297**

An example of a main idea: *Giraffes live in the Serengeti of Africa.* A supporting detail about giraffes could be: *A giraffe in the Serengeti benefits from a long neck by reaching twigs and leaves on tall trees.* The main idea gives the general idea that the text is about giraffes. The supporting detail gives a clear fact about how the giraffes eat.

A **theme** is an issue, an idea, or a question raised by a passage. For example, a theme of *Cinderella* is determination as Cinderella serves her step-sisters and step-mother. Passages may have many themes, and you must be sure to find only themes that you are asked to find. One common mark of themes is that they give more questions than answers. Authors try to push readers to consider themes in other ways. You can find themes by asking about the general problems that the passage is addressing. A good way to find a theme is to begin reading with a question in mind (e.g., How does this passage use the theme of love?) and to look for answers to that question.

> ➤ **Review Video:** <u>Theme</u>
> *Visit mometrix.com/academy and enter Code:* **732074**

Evaluating a Passage

When you read informational passages, you need to make a conclusion from the author's writing. You can **identify a logical conclusion** (i.e., find a conclusion that makes sense) to know whether you agree or disagree with an author. Coming to this conclusion is like making an inference. You combine the information from the passage with what you already know. From the passage's information and your knowledge, you can come to a conclusion that makes sense. One way to have a conclusion that makes sense is to take notes of all the author's points. When the notes are organized, they may point to the logical conclusion. Another way to reach conclusions is to ask if the author's passage raises any helpful questions. Sometimes you will be able to draw many conclusions from a passage. Yet, these may be conclusions that were never imagined by the author. Therefore, find reasons in the passage for the conclusions that you make.

> ➤ **Review Video:** Identifying a Logical Conclusion
> *Visit **mometrix.com/academy** and enter **Code: 281653***

Text evidence is the information that supports a main argument or minor argument. This evidence, or proof, can lead you to a conclusion. Information used as text evidence is clear, descriptive, and full of facts. Supporting details give evidence to back-up an argument.

For example, a passage may state that winter occurs during opposite months in the Northern hemisphere (i.e., north of the equator) and Southern hemisphere (i.e., south of the equator). Text evidence for this claim may include a list of countries where winter occurs in opposite months. Also, you may be given reasons that winter occurs at different times of the year in these hemispheres (e.g., the tilt of the Earth as it rotates around the sun).

> ➤ **Review Video:** Text Evidence
> *Visit **mometrix.com/academy** and enter **Code: 486236***

A reader should always draw conclusions from passages. Sometimes conclusions are implied (i.e., information that is assumed) from written information. Other times the information is **stated directly** within the passage. You should try to draw conclusions from information stated in a passage. Furthermore, you should always read through the entire passage before drawing conclusions. Many readers expect the author's conclusions at the beginning or the end of the passage. However, many texts do not follow this format.

Implications are things that the author does not say directly. Yet, you can assume from what the author does say. For example, *I stepped outside and opened my umbrella. By the time I got to work, the cuffs of my pants were soaked.* The author never says that it is raining. However, you can conclude that this is information is implied. Conclusions from implications must be well supported by the passage. To draw a conclusion, you should have many pieces of proof. Yet, let's say that you have only one piece. Then, you need to be sure that there is no other possible explanation than your conclusion. Practice drawing conclusions from implications in real life events to improve your skills.

Outlining the information in a passage should be a well-known skill to readers. A good outline will show the pattern of the passage and lead to better conclusions. A common outline calls for the main ideas of the passage to be listed in the order that they come. Then, beneath each main idea, you can list the minor ideas and details. An outline does not need to include every detail from the passage. However, the outline should show everything that is important to the argument.

Another helpful tool is the skill of **summarizing** information. This process is similar to creating an outline. First, a summary should define the main idea of the passage. The summary should have the most important supporting details or arguments. Summaries can be unclear or wrong because they do not stay true to the information in the passage. A helpful summary should have the same message as the passage.

Ideas from a passage can be organized using **graphic organizers**. A graphic organizer reduces information to a few key points. A graphic organizer like a timeline may have an event listed for each date on the timeline. However, an outline may have an event listed under a key point that happens in the passage.

> **Review Video: Graphic Organizers**
> Visit *mometrix.com/academy* and enter *Code:* **665513**

You need to make a graphic organizer that works best for you. Whatever helps you remember information from a passage is what you need to use. A spider-map is another example. This map takes a main idea from the story and places it in a bubble. From one main idea bubble, you put supporting points that connect to the main idea. A Venn diagram groups information as separate or connected with some overlap.

Paraphrasing is another method that you can use to understand a passage. To paraphrase, you put what you have read into your own words. Or, you can *translate* what the author shared into your words by including as many details as you can.

Responding to a Passage

One part of being a good reader is making predictions. A **prediction** is a guess about what will happen next. Readers make predictions from what they have read and what they already know. For example: *Staring at the computer screen in shock, Kim reached for the glass of water.* The sentence leaves you to think that she is not looking at the glass. So, you may guess that Kim is going to knock over the glass. Yet, in the next sentence, you may read that Kim does not knock over the glass. As you have more information, be ready for your predictions to change.

> **Review Video: Predictions**
> Visit *mometrix.com/academy* and enter *Code:* **437248**

Test-taking tip: To respond to questions that ask about predictions, your answer should come from the passage.

You will be asked to understand text that gives ideas without stating them directly. An **inference** is something that is implied but not stated directly by the author. For example: *After the final out of the inning, the fans were filled with joy and rushed the field.* From this sentence, you can infer that the fans were watching baseball and their team won. You should not use information outside of the passage before making inferences. As you practice making inferences, you will find that they need all of your attention.

> **Review Video: Inference**
> Visit *mometrix.com/academy* and enter *Code:* **379203**

Test-taking tip: When asked about inferences, look for context clues. Context is what surrounds the words and sentences that add explanation or information to an unknown piece. An answer can be *true* but not *correct*. The context clues will help you find the answer that is best. When asked for the implied meaning of a statement, you should locate the statement first. Then, read the context around the statement. Finally, look for an answer with a similar phrase.

For your exam, you must be able to find a text's **sequence** (i.e., the order that things happen). When the sequence is very important to the author, the passage comes with signal words: *first, then, next,* and *last.* However, a sequence can be implied. For example, *He walked through the garden and gave water and fertilizer to the plants.* Clearly, the man did not walk through the garden at the beginning. First, he found water. Then, he collected fertilizer. Next, he walked through the garden. Finally, he gave water and fertilizer to the plants. Passages do not always come in a clear sequence. Sometimes they begin at the end. Or, they can start over at the beginning. You can strengthen your understanding of the passage by taking notes to understand the sequence.

Building a Vocabulary

Readers of all levels will find new words in passages. The best way to define a word in **context** is to think about the words that are around the unknown word. For example, nouns that you don't know may be followed by examples that give a definition. Think about this example: *Dave arrived at the party in hilarious garb: a leopard-print shirt, buckskin pants, and tennis shoes.* If you didn't know the meaning of garb, you could read the examples (i.e., a leopard-print shirt, buckskin pants, and tennis shoes) and know that *garb* means *clothing.*

Examples will not always be this clear. Try another example: *Parsley, lemon, and flowers were just a few of items he used as garnishes.* The word *garnishes* is explained by parsley, lemon, and flowers. From this one sentence, you may know that the items are used for decoration. Are they decorating a food plate or an ice table with meat? You would need the other sentences in the paragraph to know for sure.

> **Review Video:** <u>Context</u>
> Visit **mometrix.com/academy** and enter *Code:* **613660**

Also, you can use contrasts to define an unfamiliar word in context. In many sentences, authors will not describe the unfamiliar word directly. Instead, they will describe the opposite of the unfamiliar word. So, you are given some information that will bring you closer to defining the word. For example: *Despite his intelligence, Hector's bad posture made him look obtuse. Despite* means that Hector's posture is at odds with his intelligence. The author explains that Hector's posture does not prove his intelligence. So, *obtuse* must mean *unintelligent.* Another example: *Even with the horrible weather, we were beatific about our trip to Alaska.* The weather is described as *horrible.* So, *beatific* must mean something positive.

Sometimes, there will be very few context clues to help you define an unknown word. When this happens, **substitution** is a helpful tool. First, try to think of some synonyms for the words. Then, use those synonyms in place of the unknown words. If the passage makes sense, then the substitution has given some information about the unknown word. For example: *Frank's admonition rang in her ears as she climbed the mountain.* Don't know the definition of *admonition*?

Then, try some substitutions: *vow, promise, advice, complaint,* or *compliment*. These words hint that an *admonition* is some sort of message. Once in a while substitution can get you a precise definition.

Usually, you can define an unfamiliar word by looking at the descriptive words in the context. For example: *Fred dragged the recalcitrant boy kicking and screaming up the stairs.* The words *dragged, kicking,* and *screaming* all hint that the boy hates going up the stairs. So, you may think that *recalcitrant* means something like unwilling or protesting. In this example, an unfamiliar adjective was identified.

Description is used more to define an unfamiliar noun than unfamiliar adjectives. For example: *Don's wrinkled frown and constantly shaking fist labeled him as a curmudgeon.* Don is described as having a *wrinkled frown* and *constantly shaking fist.* This hints that a *curmudgeon* must be a grumpy, old man. Contrasts do not always give detailed information about the unknown word. However, they do give you some clues to understand the word.

Many words have more than one definition. So, you may not know how the word is being used in a sentence. For example, the verb *cleave* can mean *join* or *separate*. When you see this word, you need to pick the definition that makes the most sense. For example: *The birds cleaved together as they flew from the oak tree.* The use of the word *together* hints that *cleave* is being used to mean *join*. Another example: *Hermione's knife cleaved the bread cleanly.* A knife cannot join bread together. So, the word must hint at separation. Learning the purpose of a word with many meanings needs the same tricks as defining an unknown word. Look for context clues and think about the substituted words.

Figurative Language

When authors want to share their message in a creative way, they use figurative language devices. Learning these devices will help you understand what you read. **Figurative language** is communication that goes beyond the actual meaning of a word or phrase. **Descriptive language** that awakens imagery in the reader's mind is one type of figurative language. Exaggeration is another type of figurative language. Also, when you compare two things, you are using figurative language. Similes and metaphors are the two main ways of comparing things. An example of a simile: *The child howled like a coyote when her mother told her to pick up the toys.* In this example, the child's howling is compared to a coyote. This helps the reader understand the sound being made by the child.

A **figure of speech** is a word or phrase that is not a part of straightforward, everyday language. Figures of speech are used for emphasis, fresh expression, or clearness. However, clearness of a passage may be incomplete with the use of these devices. For example: *I am going to crown you.* The author may mean:
- I am going to place a real crown on your head.
- I am going to make you king or queen of this area.
- I am going to punch you in the head with my fist.
- I am going to put a second checker's piece on top of your checker piece to show that it has become a king.

> **Review Video:** Figure of Speech
> Visit **mometrix.com/academy** and enter **Code: 111295**

Personification is the explanation of a nonhuman thing with human attributes. The basic purpose of personification is to describe something in a way that readers will understand. An author says that a tree *groans* in the wind. The author does not mean that the tree is giving a low, pained sound from a mouth.

However, the author means that the tree is making a noise like a human groan. Of course, this personification creates a tone of sadness or suffering. A different tone would be made if the author said that the tree *sways* or *dances*.

> ➤ **Review Video: Personification**
> Visit *mometrix.com/academy* and enter *Code:* **260066**

Irony is a statement that hints at the opposite of what you expect. In other words, the device is used when an author or character says one thing but means another. For example, imagine a man who is covered in mud and dressed in tattered clothes. He walks in his front door to meet his wife. Then, his wife asks him, "How was your day?" He says, "Great!" The man's response to his wife is an example of irony. There is a difference between irony and sarcasm. Sarcasm is similar to irony. However, sarcasm is hurtful for the person receiving the sarcastic statement. A sarcastic statement points to the foolishness of a person to believe that a false statement is true.

> ➤ **Review Video: Irony**
> Visit *mometrix.com/academy* and enter *Code:* **374204**

As you read, you will see more words in the context of a sentence. This will strengthen your vocabulary. Be sure to read on a regular basis. This practice will increase the number of ways that you have seen a word in context. Based on experience, a person can remember how a word was used in the past and use that knowledge for a new context. For example, a person may have seen the word *gull* used to mean a bird that is found near the seashore. However, a *gull* can be a person who is tricked easily. If the word in context is used for a person, you will see the insult. After all, gulls are not thought to be very smart. Use your knowledge of a word to find comparisons. This knowledge can be used to learn a new use of a word.

Essay

Practice Makes Prepared Writers

Writing is a skill that continues to need development throughout a person's life. For some people, writing seems to be a natural gift. They rarely struggle with writer's block. When you read their papers, they have persuasive ideas. For others, writing is an intimidating task that they endure. As you practice, you can improve your skills and be better prepared for writing a time-sensitive essay.

A traditional way to prepare for the writing section is to read. When you read newspapers, magazines, and books, you learn about new ideas. You can read newspapers and magazines to become informed about issues that affect many people. As you think about those issues and ideas, you can take a position and form opinions. Try to develop these ideas and your opinions by sharing them with friends. After you develop your opinions, try writing them down as if you were going to spread your ideas beyond your friends.

Remember that you are practicing for more than an exam. Two of the most valuable things in life are the abilities to read critically and to write clearly. When you work on evaluating the arguments of a passage and explain your thoughts well, you are developing skills that you will use for a lifetime. In this overview of essay writing, you will find strategies and tools that will prepare you to write better essays.

Essay Overview

For your exam you need to write an essay that shows your ability to understand and respond to an assignment. When you talk with others, you give beliefs, opinions, and ideas about the world around you. As you talk, you have the opportunity to share information with spoken words, facial expressions, or hand motions. If your audience seems confused about your ideas, you can stop and explain. However, when you write, you have a different assignment. As you write, you need to share information in a clear, precise way. Your readers will not have the chance to ask questions about your ideas. So, before you write your essay, you need to understand the assignment. As you write, you should be clear and precise about your ideas.

Brainstorm

Spend the first three to five minutes brainstorming for ideas. Write down any ideas that you might have on the topic. The purpose is to pull any helpful information from the depths of your memory. In this stage, anything goes down on note paper regardless of how good or bad the idea may seem at first glance. You may not bring your own paper for these notes. Instead, you will be provided with paper at the time of your test.

Strength through Different Viewpoints

The best papers will contain several examples and mature reasoning. As you brainstorm, you should consider different perspectives. There are more than two sides to every topic. In an argument, there are countless perspectives that can be considered. On any topic, different groups are impacted and many reach the same conclusion or position. Yet, they reach the same conclusion through different paths. Before writing your essay, try to *see* the topic through as many different *eyes* as you can.

In addition, you don't have to use information on how the topic impacts others. You can draw from your own experience as you wish. If you prefer to use a personal narrative, then explain the experience and your emotions from that moment. Anything that you've seen in your community can be expanded upon to round out your position on the topic.

Once you have finished with your creative flow, you need to stop and review what you brainstormed. *Which idea allowed you to come up with the most supporting information?* Be sure to pick an angle that will allow you to have a thorough coverage of the prompt.

Every garden of ideas has weeds. The ideas that you brainstormed are going to be random pieces of information of different values. Go through the pieces carefully and pick out the ones that are the best. The best ideas are strong points that will be easy to write a paragraph in response.

Now, you have your main ideas that you will focus on. So, align them in a sequence that will flow in a smooth, sensible path from point to point. With this approach, readers will go smoothly from one idea to the next in a reasonable order. Readers want an essay that has a sense of continuity (i.e., Point 1 to Point 2 to Point 3 and so on).

Start Your Engines

Now, you have a logical flow of the main ideas for the start of your essay. Begin by expanding on the first point, then move to your second point. Pace yourself. Don't spend too much time on any one of the ideas that you are expanding on. You want to have time for all of them. Make sure that you watch your time. If you have twenty minutes left to write out your ideas and you have four ideas, then you can only use five minutes per idea. Writing so much information in so little time can be an intimidating task. Yet, when you pace yourself, you can get through all of your points. If you find that you are falling behind, then you can remove one of your weaker arguments. This will allow you to give enough support to your remaining paragraphs.

Once you finish expanding on an idea, go back to your brainstorming session where you wrote out your ideas. You can scratch through the ideas as you write about them. This will let you see what you need to write about next and what you have left to cover.

Your introductory paragraph should have several easily identifiable features.
- First, the paragraph should have a quick description or paraphrasing of the topic. Use your own words to briefly explain what the topic is about.
- Second, you should list your writing points. What are the main ideas that you came up with earlier? If someone was to read only your introduction, they should be able to get a good summary of the entire paper.
- Third, you should explain your opinion of the topic and give an explanation for why you feel that way. What is your decision or conclusion on the topic?

Each of your following paragraphs should develop one of the points listed in the main paragraph. Use your personal experience and knowledge to support each of your points. Examples should back up everything.

Once you have finished expanding on each of your main points, you need to conclude your essay. Summarize what you written in a conclusion paragraph. Explain once more your argument on the prompt and review why you feel that way in a few sentences. At this stage, you have already backed up your statements. So, there is no need to do that again. You just need to refresh your readers on the main points that you made in your essay.

Don't Panic

Whatever you do during essay, do not panic. When you panic, you will put fewer words on the page and your ideas will be weak. Therefore, panicking is not helpful. If your mind goes blank when you see the prompt, then you need to take a deep breath. Force yourself to go through the steps listed above: brainstorm and put anything on scratch paper that comes to mind.

Also, don't get clock fever. You may be overwhelmed when you're looking at a page that has is mostly blank. Your mind is full of random thoughts and feeling confused, and the clock is ticking down faster. You have already brainstormed for ideas. Therefore, you don't have to keep coming up with ideas. If you're running out of time and you have a lot of ideas that you haven't written down, then don't be afraid to make some cuts. Start picking the best ideas that you have left and expand on them. Don't feel like you have to write on all of your ideas.

A short paper that is well written and well organized is better than a long paper that is poorly written and poorly organized. Don't keep writing about a subject just to add sentences and avoid repeating a statement or idea that you have explained already. The goal is 1 to 2 pages of quality writing. That is your target, but you should not mess up your paper by trying to get there. You want to have a natural end to your work without having to cut something short. If your essay is a little long, then that isn't a problem as long as your ideas are clear and flow well from paragraph to paragraph. Just be sure that your writing stays inside the assigned borders of the papers. Remember to expand on the ideas that you identified in the brainstorming session.

Leave time at the end (at least three minutes) to go back and check over your work. Reread and make sure that everything you've written makes sense and flows well. Clean up any spelling or grammar mistakes. Also, go ahead and erase any brainstorming ideas that you weren't able to include. Then, clean up any extra information that you might have written that doesn't fit into your paper.

As you proofread, make sure that there aren't any fragments or run-ons. Check for sentences that are too short or too long. If the sentence is too short, then look to see if you have a specific subject and an active verb. If it is too long, then break up the long sentence into two sentences. Watch out for any "big words" that you may have used. Be sure that you are using difficult words correctly. Don't misunderstand; you should try to increase your vocabulary and use difficult words in your essay. However, your focus should be on developing and expressing ideas in a clear and precise way.

The Short Overview

Depending on your preferences and personality, the essay may be your hardest or your easiest section. You are required to go through the entire process of writing a paper in a limited amount of time which is very challenging.

Stay focused on each of the steps for brainstorming. Go through the process of creative flow first. You can start by generating ideas about the prompt. Next, organize those ideas into a smooth flow. Then, pick out the ideas that are the best from your list.

Create a recognizable essay structure in your paper. Start with an introduction that explains what you have decided to argue. Then, choose your main points. Use the body paragraphs to touch on those main points and have a conclusion that wraps up the topic.

Save a few moments to go back and review what you have written. Clean up any minor mistakes that you might have made and make those last few critical touches that can make a huge difference. Finally, be proud and confident of what you have written!

Practice Test

Section 1 – Verbal Reasoning

Each of the following questions consists of one word followed by four words. Select the one word whose meaning is closest to the word in capital letters. You are not allowed to use scrap paper, a dictionary, or a thesaurus.

Part One – Synonyms

1. INSTRUCTOR
   a. dictator
   b. pupil
   c. survivor
   d. teacher

2. INSTANTLY
   a. definitely
   b. eventually
   c. immediately
   d. reluctantly

3. GIGANTIC
   a. harsh
   b. huge
   c. scary
   d. small

4. COSTLY
   a. attractive
   b. cheap
   c. expensive
   d. rare

5. FREQUENTLY
   a. difficulty
   b. easy
   c. freely
   d. often

6. OBSERVED
   a. hunted
   b. scared
   c. sold
   d. watched

- 48 -

7. PURCHASED
   a. bargained
   b. bought
   c. complained
   d. sold

8. ENTIRE
   a. basic
   b. divide
   c. tired
   d. whole

9. SUPERIOR
   a. better
   b. short
   c. similar
   d. weak

10. SELECTING
    a. choosing
    b. contacting
    c. informing
    d. locating

11. SWIFTLY
    a. lightly
    b. quickly
    c. slowly
    d. surely

12. CHUCKLED
    a. chose
    b. commented
    c. helped
    d. laughed

13. LOCATE
    a. buy
    b. enjoy
    c. find
    d. share

14. PUZZLED
    a. admired
    b. confused
    c. retired
    d. understand

15. CHEAP
    a. cheat
    b. cheer
    c. doubtfully
    (d.) inexpensive

16. INTELLIGENT
    a. mysterious
    b. nice
    c. pretty
    (d.) smart

17. REQUIRED
    (a.) needed
    b. studied
    c. wanted
    d. wished

Part Two – Sentence Completion

DIRECTIONS: Select the answer choice that best completes the sentence. You are not allowed to use scrap paper, a dictionary, or a thesaurus.

18. The pop star wore a disguise and exited through a back door to avoid being _____ by the paparazzi.
    a. humiliated
    b. ignored
    c. overlooked
    (d.) welcomed

19. The fashion expert _____ Sylvia's apparel as being out of date.
    a. applauded
    b. drafted
    c. praised
    (d.) rejected

20. The others were not upset by Steve's strange behavior, as they were _____ with it.
    a. acquainted → familiar with
    (b.) appalled ⎤
    c. disgusted ⎦ Synonyms
    d. unfamiliar

21. Ned's clumsy handling of the garden hose caused poor little Ike to be _____.
    a. drenched
    b. dry
    c. entertained
    d. unaffected

22. That message I sent was intended _____ for you and not all of your friends.
    a. commonly
    b. expressly — *specifically, particularly*
    c. generally
    d. possibly

23. James exclaimed dramatically, "I'm so _____ that I could eat an immense meal!"
    a. congested
    b. nauseated
    c. satisfied
    d. starved

24. When he slid quietly out of his desk, the student _____ his things and left the room.
    a. collected
    b. delayed
    c. disciplined
    d. hoisted

25. When he discovered his fiancée's lies, his _____ reaction was to discount her request for trust.
    a. illegible
    b. instantaneous
    c. luscious
    d. unpredictable

26. The inventor found a(n) _____ method to resolve his product's design problem.
    a. awkward
    b. clever
    c. incompetent
    d. ingenuous

profitable, money making

27. Glenda was _____ disability benefits because she had gainful employment.
    a. assigned
    b. given
    c. granted
    d. refused

28. Be forewarned that students who talk during her lectures particularly _____ this teacher.
    a. aid
    b. delight
    c. irritate
    d. soothe

29. Sue had _____ that the delicious meal would later give her digestive problems.
    a. anxieties
    b. diffused
    c. enshrined
    d. hopes

30. The low temperatures and high winds in the blizzard changed the difficult _____ for the campers.
   a. audition
   b. journey
   c. mortgage
   d. suffrage

31. How she could manipulate a child so shamelessly is _____ to me.
   a. admirable
   b. intolerable
   c. maternal
   d. prodigal

32. The discomfort you are feeling could be one of the _____ effects of your new medication.
   a. beneficial
   b. conflicting
   c. desirable
   d. useful

33. Accusations that the public figure was a(n) _____ man were, happily, proven to be false.
   a. commendable
   b. deceitful
   c. heroic
   d. pleasant

34. You can't be objective about your own work, so have a _____ third party look at it.
   a. biased
   b. disinterested
   c. prejudiced
   d. revolutionary

Section 2 -- Quantitative Reasoning

In this section there are four possible answers after each question. Choose which one is best.
You are not allowed a calculator, a calculator watch, a ruler, a protractor, or a compass.

1. The figure shows an irregular quadrilateral and the lengths of its sides. Which of the following equations best shows the perimeter of the quadrilateral?

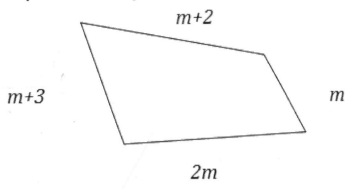

a. $m^4 + 5$
b. $2m^4 + 5$
c. $4m + 5$
d. $5m + 5$

2. Of the 20 people in Joan's class, 4 of them have birthdays in the winter, 7 have birthdays in the spring, 3 have birthdays in the summer, and 6 have birthdays in the fall. What is the probability a student chosen at random will have a birthday in either the spring or the summer?

a. $\frac{3}{20}$

b. $\frac{3}{10}$

c. $\frac{7}{20}$

d. $\frac{1}{2}$

3. A rectangular plot in a garden is three times longer than it is wide. What is the perimeter of the garden if it has a width of 8 meters?

a. 24 meters
b. 32 meters
c. 64 meters
d. 192 meters

- 53 -

4. The figure below is divided into cubes. Each cube has a volume of 1 unit³. What is the volume of this figure?

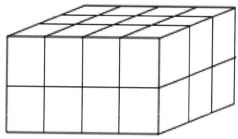

a. 12 units
b. 16 units
c. 18 units
d. 24 units

5. Which of the following correctly describes the relationship between the values of x and y, as shown in the table below?

x	y
1	4
2	8
3	12
4	16

a. The value of x is 6 less than the value of y
b. The value of y is 4 times the value of x
c. The value of y is 4 more than the value of x
d. The value of x is 1 less than the value of y

6. A bag full of C cookies is equally distributed among S students. Which expression correctly determines the number of cookies each student receives?
a. $C \div S$
b. $C \times S$
c. $C - S$
d. $S \div C$

7. Harlan plans to make stew for a large group. The recipe he uses requires 150 carrots. He knows that he can buy large bags of carrots for $3.75 each. What additional information does Harlan need to find the amount of money the carrots will cost for his stew?
a. The amounts of other vegetables he will need for the stew
b. The number of people he expects to eat the stew
c. The price each person attending the event paid
d. The number of carrots in a large bag of carrots

8. Which of the following is correct?

a. $\frac{4}{7} = \frac{12}{21}$

b. $\frac{3}{4} = \frac{12}{20}$

c. $\frac{5}{8} = \frac{15}{32}$

d. $\frac{7}{9} = \frac{28}{35}$

9. The graph below shows Aaron's distance from home at times throughout his morning run. Which of the following statements is (are) true?

I. Aaron's average running speed was 6 mph.

II. Aaron's running speed from point A to point B was the same as his running speed from point D to E.

III. Aaron ran a total distance of four miles.

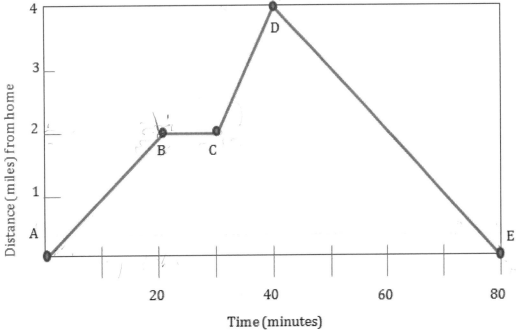

Time (minutes)

a. I only

b. II only

c. I and II

d. I, II, and III

10. An electronics store sells E Evercell brand batteries in packages of 4 and D Durapower brand batteries in packages of 6. Which expression represents the total number of batteries in the store?

a. $(4 + E) \times (6 + D)$

b. $(4 \times E) + (6 \times D)$

c. $(4 + E) + (6 + D)$

d. $(4 \times E) \div (6 \times D)$

11. A woman wants to park her 15 foot long car in a garage that is 19 feet long. How far from the front of the garage will her front wheels need to be so that the car is centered on the floor of the garage?

 a. 2 feet

 b. $2\frac{1}{2}$ feet

 c. 3 feet

 d. $3\frac{1}{2}$ feet

12. Two sets of numbers are shown here. In each set, the terms increase by the same amount each time.

 Set M = {1, 4, 7, 10, 13, ...}

 Set V = {1, 3, 5, 7, 9, ...}

What is the first number greater than 20 which is a member of both Set M and Set V?

 a. 21

 b. 23

 c. 25

 d. 27

13. Solve for x:

4x + 4 = 36

 a. -11

 b. -8

 c. 5

 d. 8

14. Cindy earned $100 one week at the ice cream stand. She put $\frac{1}{4}$ of the money in her savings account and kept the rest as cash. After this, she received a cash bonus of $20 from the owner of the ice cream stand and didn't put any of it in the savings account. Which expression represents the amount of cash Cindy currently has?

 a. $C = \frac{3}{4}(100) + 20$

 b. $C = \frac{1}{4}(100) + 20$

 c. $C = \frac{1}{4}(100) - 2$

 d. $C = \frac{3}{4}(120)$

15. Which of the following shapes do not have a line symmetry?

 a.   b.

 c.   d.

- 56 -

16. Which one of the statements about the cube below is FALSE?

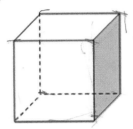

    a. There are 12 edges on the cube.
    b. All edges are the same length.
    c. Some of the edges are parallel.
    d. None of the edges are perpendicular.

17. Which statement about the shaded region of the two figures is true?
    a. Figure A is greater than Figure B
    b. Figure A is less than Figure B
    c. Figure A is equal to figure B
    d. No comparison can be made

Figure A   Figure B

18. Jackson can decorate a cake in 3 hours. Eli can decorate the same cake in 2 hours. If they work together, how long will it take them to decorate the cake?
    a. 0.8 hours
    b. 1.2 hours
    c. 1.5 hours
    d. 1.8 hours

19. Two sisters were arguing who could have a larger piece of pie. Their mother told the older daughter she could have 2/5 of the pie. She told the younger daughter she could have 1/3 of the pie. Which daughter received a larger piece of pie?
    a. The older daughter.
    b. The younger daughter
    c. Same size piece for each daughter
    d. Not enough information to determine

$$\frac{6}{15} \qquad \frac{5}{15}$$

20. A wealthy uncle decides to give away half of his fortune. Each of his 5 relatives is to receive an equal share. Which of the statements below describes how this can be done?
    a. Multiply his wealth by 1/5 and give this amount to each of his relatives
    b. Multiply his wealth by 1/2 and give this amount to each of his relatives
    c. Multiply his wealth by 1/10 and give this amount to each of his relatives
    d. Multiply his wealth by 2/5 and give this amount to each of his relatives

21. Which method below is NOT correct for finding the amount owed if three items are purchased at $3.99 each?

   a. $3 \times 4 - 3 \times 0.01$
   b. $3.99 \div 3$
   c. $3 \times 3 + 3 \times 0.9 + 3 \times 0.09$
   d. $3.99 + 3.99 + 3.99$

22. Which line is a line of symmetry for the figure?

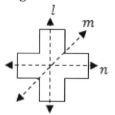

   a. Line l
   b. Line m
   c. Line n
   d. All of the above

23. Which of the following is the largest number?

   a. 0.004
   b. 0.400
   c. 0.2
   d. 0.03

24. The table below shows changes in the area of several trapezoids as the lengths of the bases, b_1 and b_2, remain the same and the height, h, changes.

Trapezoids

b_1 (in feet)	b_2 (in feet)	h (in feet)	A (in square feet)
5	7	2	12
5	7	4	24
5	7	6	36
5	7	8	48

Which formula best represents the relationship between A, the areas of these trapezoids, and h, their heights?

   a. $A = 5h$
   b. $A = 6h$
   c. $A = 7h$
   d. $A = 12h$

25. Alma collected coins. In the bag where she kept only dimes, she had dimes from four different years. She had 20 dimes minted in 1942, 30 minted in 1943, 40 minted in 1944, and 10 minted in 1945. If Alma reached into the bag without looking and took a dime, what is the probability that she took a dime minted in 1945?

    a. $\frac{1}{10}$

    b. $\frac{1}{5}$

    c. $\frac{3}{10}$

    d. $\frac{2}{5}$

26. Jason wants to put dry fertilizer on the grass in his front yard. The yard is 20 feet wide and 45 feet long. Each pound of the fertilizer he plans to use is enough for 150 square feet. Which procedure could Jason use to determine the correct amount of fertilizer to use on the entire yard?

    a. Divide 150 by 20 and divide 150 by 45, and then add those quotients together
    b. Add 20 and 45, double that total, and then divide that total by 150
    c. Multiply 20 by 45, and then subtract 150 from that product
    d. Multiply 20 by 45, and then divide that product by 150

27. Antonio wants to buy a roll of border to finish an art project. At four different shops, he found four different borders he liked. He wants to use the widest of the borders. The list shows the width, in inches, of the borders he found.

$$1\frac{7}{10} , 1.72 , 1\frac{3}{4} , 1.695$$

Which roll of border should Antonio buy if he wants to buy the widest border?

    a. $1\frac{7}{10}$
    b. 1.72
    c. $1\frac{3}{4}$
    d. 1.695

28. Glenda poured salt into three salt shakers from a box that contained 26 ounces of salt. She poured 2 ounces of salt into one shaker, 3 ounces of salt into the second shaker, and 4 ounces into the third shaker. She did not pour salt into any other shakers. Which expression best represents the amount of salt left in the box after Glenda poured salt into the three shakers?

    a. 2 – 3 – 4 + 26
    b. 2 + 3 + 4 – 26
    c. 26 – 2 + 3 + 4
    d. 26 – 2 – 3 – 4

29. In $\triangle RST$, shown here, $m\angle S$ is 20° less than $m\angle R$.

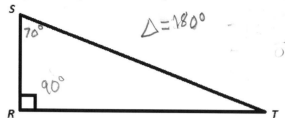

What is the measure of $\angle T$?
   a. 20°
   b. 50°
   c. 70°
   d. 110°

30. The drawing shows a window with equal-sized panes. Some of the panes are not tinted, some are tinted a light shade of gray, and some are tinted a very dark shade of gray.

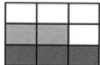

Which number sentence best models the total section of the window that has tinted panes?
   a. $\frac{1}{3} + \frac{1}{3} = \frac{2}{3}$
   b. $\frac{1}{3} + \frac{2}{9} = \frac{5}{9}$
   c. $\frac{1}{9} + \frac{2}{3} = \frac{7}{9}$
   d. $\frac{2}{9} + \frac{4}{9} = \frac{2}{3}$

31. Jeff saw 25 cars in the school parking lot. If each car brought from 1 to 3 people to school, which is the best estimate of the total number of people arriving to school in the 25 cars?
   a. 25
   b. 50
   c. 75
   d. 100

32. One morning at Jim's café, 25 people ordered juice, 10 ordered milk, and 50 ordered coffee with breakfast. Which ratio best compares the number of people who ordered milk to the number of people who ordered juice?
   a. 5 to 7
   b. 5 to 2
   c. 2 to 7
   d. 2 to 5

- 60 -

33. A unit of liquid measure in the English System of Measure is the gill. The table, shown here, gives conversions from gills to fluid ounces.

Conversion Table

Gills	Fluid Ounces
2	8
4	16
5	20
6	24
10	40

Which equation best describes the relationship between gills, g, and fluid ounces, f?
   a. $f = 8g - 8$
   b. $f = 2g + 4$
   c. $f = 4g$
   d. $4f = g$

34. A trash company charges a fee of \$80 to haul off a load of trash. There is also a charge of \$0.05 per mile the load must be hauled. Which equation can be used to find c, the cost for hauling a load of trash m miles?
   a. $80(m + 0.05)$
   b. $0.05(m + 80)$
   c. $80m + 0.05$
   d. $0.05m + 80$

35. Which of these is **NOT** a net of a cube?
   a.   b.   c.   d.

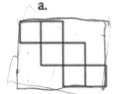 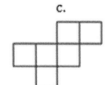 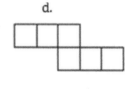

36. Which of the following statements is true?
   a. The measure of an acute angle is greater than the measure of a right angle, but less than the measure of an obtuse angle
   b. The measure of a right angle is greater than the measure of an acute angle, but less than the measure of an obtuse angle
   c. The measure of an obtuse angle is less than the measure of a right angle, but greater than the measure of an acute angle
   d. The measure of an obtuse angle is less than the measure of an acute angle, but greater than the measure of a right angle

37. The number of customers in a new restaurant is given in the table below:

Week	Customers
1	155
2	180
3	205

How many customers should be expected in week 4?
 a. 200
 b. 225
 c. 230
 d. 255

38. An elevator leaves the first floor of a 25-story building with 3 people on board. It stops at every floor. Each time it comes to an even-numbered floor, 3 people get on and one person gets off. Each time it comes to an odd-numbered floor, 3 people get on and 4 people get off. How many people are on board when it arrives at the 25th floor?
 a. 12
 b. 13
 c. 15
 d. 16

$$1 \overset{st}{=} 2$$
$$2 \overset{nd}{=} 4$$
$$3 \overset{rd}{=} 6$$

Section 3 – Reading Comprehension

You are not allowed to use scrap paper, a dictionary, or a thesaurus.

The Tournament

1   The Knights led by two points, and Scott was just outside the three-point line. If
2   he could make the shot, the Eagles would be state champions again. But if he missed …
3   Scott didn't want to think about that. He knew what he had to do.

4   It was a classic jump shot. The ball left his hands and sailed toward the basket in a
5   perfect arc. The crowd and the other players seemed frozen in time. All eyes were on
6   the ball as it struck the rim and bounced off. The buzzer blared. The game was over.
7   Scott had missed, and the Eagles had lost.

8   Scott stood like a statue on the court as people surged around him. Family members
9   swarmed the winning team. Teammates hugged and patted each other on the back.
10   Local reporters gathered around the Knights head coach for a comment and a
11   photograph.

12   Suddenly, Scott realized that he was being hoisted onto the shoulders of his friends. 13   Over the
loudspeaker, the announcer had proclaimed that Scott had been named the
14   most valuable player of the championship game. Everyone was elated, and the Eagles
15   took a victory lap with Scott on their shoulders.

16   Scott was confused as his teammates set him down. He was the one who missed the
17   most important shot of the game. How could anyone call him the most valuable player?
18   He didn't feel very valuable at the moment. Scott approached Coach Travis.

19   "Coach," Scott said, "there must be some mistake. I can't be the most valuable
20   player."

21   "There's no mistake," Coach Travis said. "You had 26 points, 11 rebounds, and 8
22   assists. I'd say that makes you a very valuable player."

23   "But I missed that last shot," Scott said. "We lost the game because of me."

24   "I don't know about that," said Coach Travis. "Everybody misses a shot from time to
25   time. Don't be so hard on yourself. It's all depends on how you look at the outcome."

26   "What do you mean?" Scott asked.

27   "Well," Coach Travis answered, "you could say you are the reason we lost the game
28   because you missed that shot. On the other hand, you could say you are the reason we
29   almost won because of your performance throughout the game. How you look at it is up
30   to you."

31   Scott's teammates came running over and surrounded Coach Travis. "Hey, Coach,"
32   one player called out, "how about treating your team to pizza?"

33   "I don't know," said Coach Travis. "Do you think you deserve pizza?"

34   Scott piped up. "Of course we do! After all, we almost won the game."

35   Coach Travis smiled. "You're right, Scott. We did almost win. Okay. Pizza for
36   everyone!"

1. In line 14, what does "elated" mean?
   a. Happy and excited
   b. Frustrated and angry
   c. Loud and rowdy
   d. Pushy and proud

2. In line 8, what type of figurative language is used?
   a. Hyperbole
   b. Metaphor
   c. Personification
   d. Simile

3. Which of the following best expresses the theme of this story?
   a. The Eagles want to be the state champions
   b. There are different ways to look at any situation
   c. Winning isn't everything
   d. Scott is a very good basketball player

4. Which of the following is the best summary of this story?
   a. At the buzzer, Scott misses an important basket because he isn't a very good basketball player
   b. Coach Travis feels Scott is the most valuable player in the game because he scored 26 points
   c. When Scott misses an important shot, he is disappointed, but Coach Travis shows him there are different ways to look at the situation
   d. The Eagles lose the state championship because of Scott, but Coach Travis sees things differently and makes Scott the most valuable player

5. Why is Scott so upset in this story?
   a. He feels responsible for losing the game
   b. He thinks he is a bad basketball player
   c. He doesn't like Coach Travis
   d. He doesn't want to play basketball anymore

The Tradition of Dance

1   It is estimated that there are over 300 Native American tribes, and each of them
2 uses dancing to communicate culture. Native American dances date back hundreds of
3 years and come in many different forms. Different tribes use dance for different
4 purposes and to convey different messages.

5   Although each dance is different, they all have meanings that are rooted in ancient
6 tradition. The Iroquois performed a corn husk dance to bring good crops and many
7 healthy babies to the tribe. The Choctaw women danced with medicine men to bring
8 their tribe victory in sporting events. The Plains Indians offered thanks to the gods
9 through their Sun Dance, and the Cherokee celebrated both peace and war with the
10 Eagle Dance. During the Snake Ceremonial, Hopi dancers even held live snakes in their
11 mouths before releasing them into the desert to bring rain and a good harvest.

12   Each of the many different dances also requires a unique costume. These costumes
13 vary widely, but—just like the dances—each has a special meaning. Most dance
14 costumes include a headdress and special ceremonial clothing. Some also include a
15 wand, jewelry, and even body paint. In addition, feathers are often used in costumes to
16 symbolize human traits. One of the most common feathers used is the eagle feather,
17 which represents strength in many tribes.

18   Though many of the Native American dances are now performed only in ceremonies
19 and at powwows, they remain an important element of Native American culture. These
20 dances are a language, rich in history and meaning. They are passed from generation to
21 generation and will always be a vital part of Native American tradition.

6. What is the main purpose of dance in the Native American culture?
    a. To provide exercise
    b. To communicate a message
    c. To entertain children
    d. To prepare for battle

7. According to paragraph 2 (lines 5-11), what is the similarity between the Iroquois corn husk dance and the Hopi Snake Ceremonial?
    a. They were both intended to bring good crops
    b. They both involved women and medicine men
    c. They both involved the use of snakes
    d. They both involved the use of corn husks

8. Which of the following is a statement of fact?
    a. Eagle feathers are the best feathers
    b. Native American costumes are beautiful
    c. Ceremonial headdresses make dancers look important
    d. Many Native American costumes include a wand and jewelry

9. What does the eagle feather represent in many Native American tribes?
    a. Power
    b. Wealth
    c. Strength
    d. Authority

10. What was the author's main purpose in writing this article?
    a. To inform
    b. To entertain
    c. To influence
    d. To persuade

The Giant Sequoia

1   Most people think that the Giant Sequoia (*Sequoiadendron giganteum*) is the largest
2 living organism. This conifer grows mostly in groves located in the Sierra Nevada
3 Mountains in California. The biggest single Giant Sequoia is called the General Sherman
4 tree. The General Sherman is 250 feet tall and has a diameter of 24.75 feet at the
5 bottom. The trunk of this massive tree weighs nearly 1400 tons. That's about the weight
6 of 10 trains or 15 fully grown blue whales.

7   But some people do not think that labeling the Giant Sequoia as the largest living
8 organism is correct. That is because the majority of the material that makes up a tree is
9 made up of dead cells rather than living matter. In addition, there are other types of
10 plants that reproduce in such a way that they are connected with roots under the
11 ground, such as a grove of aspen trees or a field of goldenrod flowers. Some people
12 think that these large, connected groves should be considered the largest organism. In
13 any case, a Giant Sequoia is indeed a massive and beautiful sight to behold indeed.

11. Based on the context of this passage, what is a conifer?
    a. an animal
    b. a tree
    c. a flower
    d. a cell

12. Is the Giant Sequoia the largest organism?
    a. yes
    b. no
    c. some people think it is
    d. most people think so

13. What is the General Sherman?
    a. the biggest train
    b. the largest connected organism
    c. the largest Giant Sequoia
    d. a type of whale

14. Why do some people think that a grove of aspen trees should be considered the largest organism?
    a. because the trees are taller
    b. because the trees have a wider diameter
    c. because the grove is connected underneath the ground
    d. because there are more of them in the United States

15. What is the diameter of the General Sherman tree at the top?
    a. 15 feet
    b. 20 feet
    c. 24.75 feet
    d. This question cannot be answered from the information given

Remember the Alamo

1   In the early 1700s, the Spanish established missions throughout the land we now
2 know as the state of Texas. One of the most famous of these missions was San Antonio
3 de Valero, better known by its nickname: the Alamo. This was the most successful
4 mission in the area, and it served a number of purposes for the surrounding
5 communities.

6   For over a century, the Alamo served as an active mission. Church services were
7 held in the cool, shady buildings, providing welcome relief from the blazing summer
8 sun. Couples were married at the Alamo. Babies were baptized there. The Alamo also
9 served as a trading post, supply depot, and communication center. In later years,
10 however, the Alamo served its most famous and—arguably—most important role; it
11 was a fortress for freedom fighters.

12   During the 1830s, Texas was in a battle for independence from Mexico, which
13 owned it at that time. This struggle came to a head in 1836 when 184 Texans, led by
14 William Travis, holed up in the Alamo. Travis and other famous American fighters—
15 including Jim Bowie and Davy Crockett—fought side by side with farmers, ranchers,
16 cowboys, and businessmen. Those brave men held off Mexican General Santa Anna's
17 army for 13 days from the secure walls of the Alamo.

18   Finally, in the gray, early morning light of March 6, 1836, General Santa Anna and an
19 army of 4,000 soldiers overran the Alamo. Every man in the Alamo died that day, but
20 their ability to hold out for nearly two weeks gave American General Sam Houston the
21 time he needed to assemble a more substantial army. General Houston soon defeated
22 General Santa Anna, and Texas won its independence, thanks in great part to the brave
23 men who defended the Alamo and the cause of freedom.

16. What was the official name of the mission nicknamed "the Alamo"?
    a. San Antonio de Valente
    b. San Antonio de Verde
    c. San Antonio de Valero
    d. San Antonio de Vallejo

17. Which of the following represents the author's main purpose in writing this story?
    a. To inform
    b. To influence
    c. To entertain
    d. To persuade

18. What was the main motivation for the men who fought at the Alamo?
    a. Wealth
    b. Fame
    c. Safety
    d. Freedom

19. Based on the information in paragraph 2 (lines 6-11), what was the purpose of the Alamo?
    a. It was designed as a war fortress
    b. It was designed to serve many purposes in the community
    c. It was designed as a trading post
    d. It was designed as a saloon

20. Which of the following is a statement of opinion?
    a. William Travis, Davy Crockett, and Jim Bowie fought at the Alamo
    b. All the men who fought to defend the Alamo died in the battle
    c. General Santa Anna was eventually defeated by General Sam Houston
    d. General Santa Anna was a better leader than William Travis

Cultivation of Tomato Plants

1   Tomato plants should be started in window boxes or greenhouses in late March so
2 that they will be ready for the garden after the last frost. Use a soil of equal parts of
3 sand, peat moss and manure, and plant the seeds about a quarter of an inch deep. After
4 covering, water them through a cloth to protect the soil and cover the box with a pane
5 of glass. Keep the box in a warm place for a few days, then place it in a sunny window.
6 After the second leaf makes its appearance on the seedling, transplant the plant to
7 another box, placing the seedlings two inches apart. Another alternative is to put the
8 sprouted seedlings in four-inch pots, setting them deeper in the soil than they stood in
9 the seed bed. To make the stem stronger, pinch out the top bud when the seedlings are
10 four or five inches in height.

11   Finally, place the plants in their permanent positions after they have grown to be
12 twelve or fifteen inches high. When transplanting, parts of some of the longest leaves
13 should be removed. Large plants may be set five or six inches deep.

14   The soil should be fertilized the previous season. Fresh, stable manure, used as
15 fertilizer, would delay the time of fruiting. To improve the condition of the soil, work in
16 a spade full of old manure to a depth of at least a foot. Nitrate of soda, applied at about
17 two hundred pounds per acre, may be used to give the plant a good start.

18   Plants grown on supports may be set two feet apart in the row, with the rows three
19 or four feet apart depending upon the variety. Plants not supported by stakes or other
20 methods should be set four feet apart.

21   Unsupported vines give a lighter yield and much of the fruit is likely to rot during
22 the wet seasons. Use well sharpened stakes about two inches in diameter and five feet
23 long. Drive the stakes into the ground at least six inches from the plants so that the
24 roots will not be injured. Tie the tomato vines to the stakes with strings made out of
25 strips of cloth, as twine is likely to cut them. Care must be taken not to wrap the limbs
26 so tightly as to interfere with their growth. The training should start before the plants
27 begin to trail on the ground.

21. What is the overall purpose of this passage?
    a. To describe how soil should be treated in order to plant tomatoes.
    b. To give an overview of how tomato plants are cultured.
    c. To teach the reader how to operate a farm.
    d. To describe a method of supporting tomato vines.

22. According to the passage, why is late March the best time to germinate tomato seeds?
    a. The last frost has already passed by this time.
    b. It is warm enough by then to germinate them in window boxes.
    c. By the time the last frost passes, they will be ready to transplant outdoors.
    d. The seeds might not be fertile if one were to wait longer.

23. What does the passage imply as the reason that the seeds not planted outdoors immediately?
    a. A late freeze might kill the seedlings.
    b. The soil outdoors is too heavy for new seedlings.
    c. A heavy rain might wash away the seedlings.
    d. New seedlings need to be close to one another and then be moved apart later.

24. What would happen if the bud weren't pinched out of the seedlings when they are in individual pots?
    a. The plants would be weaker.
    b. The plants would freeze.
    c. The plants would need more water.
    d. The plants would not survive as long.

25. What is the purpose of the last paragraph?
    a. To explain why unsupported plants give rotten fruit.
    b. To explain why cloth is used rather than wire.
    c. To describe in detail how tomato plants are cultured.
    d. To instruct the reader in the method of supporting tomato vines for culture.

Section 4 – Mathematics Achievement

In this section there are four possible answers after each question. Choose which one is best. You are not allowed a calculator, a calculator watch, a ruler, a protractor, or a compass.

1. Janice gets home from school at 2:45 PM. She does homework for 1 hour and 30 minutes, then goes out and plays for 1 hour and 45 minutes before returning home for dinner. What time is it when Janice returns home for dinner?

a.

b.

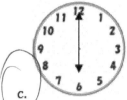
c.

d.

2. What is the value of the digit 5 in the number 3,456,789?
   a. Fifty thousand
   b. Five thousand
   c. Five-hundred thousand
   d. Five million

3. What is the 14th number in the pattern shown below?
100, 200, 300, 400, ...
   a. 1,200
   b. 1,300
   c. 1,400
   d. 1,500

4. The recipe Mary is using to bake cupcakes requires 1 cup of milk and makes 8 cupcakes. If she needs to make 32 cupcakes for the party, how much milk is needed?
   a. 1 pint
   b. 1 gallon
   c. 3 cups
   d. 1 quart

5. Matthew wants to buy a video game that costs $25. He only has $18. How much additional money does Matthew need to save to purchase the game?
   a. $5
   b. $6
   c. $7
   d. $8

6. Julie shopped for first-aid cream. One large tube held 1.5 fluid ounces and the smallest tube held 0.33 fluid ounces. What is the difference in the number of fluid ounces of cream in the two tubes?
   a. 1.17
   b. 1.23
   c. 1.27
   d. 1.8

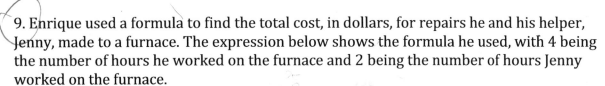

7. 3.5 + 10.3 + 0.63 =
   a. 11.28
   b. 13.58
   c. 14.43
   d. 20.10

8. Large boxes of canned beans hold 24 cans of beans and small boxes hold 12 cans. One afternoon, Gerald brought 4 large boxes of canned beans and 6 small boxes of canned beans to the food bank. How many cans of beans did Gerald bring to the food bank that afternoon?
   a. 168
   b. 192
   c. 288
   d. 360

9. Enrique used a formula to find the total cost, in dollars, for repairs he and his helper, Jenny, made to a furnace. The expression below shows the formula he used, with 4 being the number of hours he worked on the furnace and 2 being the number of hours Jenny worked on the furnace.

   $20 + 35(4 + 2) + 47$

What is the total cost for repairing the furnace?
   a. $189
   b. $269
   c. $277
   d. $377

- 71 -

10. What is the equivalent decimal number for six hundred six thousandths?
   a. .0606
   b. .606
   c. 6.006
   d. 6.600

11. Jan played a game which used a fair spinner like the one shown here. Jan needs the arrow to land on green on her next turn.

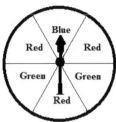

What is the probability that the arrow lands on green when Jan spins one time?

   a. $\frac{1}{6}$

   b. $\frac{1}{3}$

   c. $\frac{1}{2}$

   d. $\frac{2}{3}$

12. What decimal is represented by Point P, shown on the number line below?

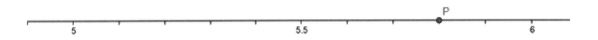

   a. 5.6
   b. 5.7
   c. 5.8
   d. 5.9

13. Simplify $4\frac{1}{3} - 2\frac{2}{3}$.

   a. $1\frac{1}{9}$

   b. $1\frac{2}{3}$

   c. $2\frac{1}{3}$

   d. $2\frac{3}{6}$

- 72 -

14. Stephen researched the topic of solar-powered lights for his science project. He exposed 10 new solar lights to five hours of sunlight. He recorded the number of minutes each light continued to shine after dark in the list below.

63, 67, 73, 75, 80, 91, 63, 72, 79, 87

Which of these numbers is the mean of the number of minutes in Stephen's list?
 a. 28
 b. 63
 c. 74
 d. 75

15. Petra installed 10 light fixtures at a new warehouse that was being built. Each of the fixtures required 3 light bulbs. The bulbs come in packages of 5 and cost $8 per package. What was the total cost for the bulbs required for all of the fixtures Petra installed at the warehouse?
 a. $16
 b. $48
 c. $120
 d. $240

16. Where would the answer to $\frac{4}{5} - \frac{1}{16}$ lie on the number line below?

a. between 0 and $\frac{1}{4}$

b. between $\frac{1}{4}$ and $\frac{1}{2}$

c. between $\frac{1}{2}$ and $\frac{3}{4}$

d. between $\frac{3}{4}$ and 1

17. What type of transformation is represented by the two figures below?

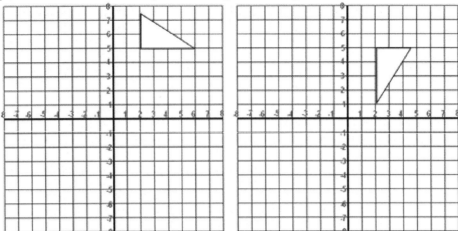

    a. Reflection
    b. Translation
    c. Rotation
    d. None of these

18. Which of the following is the written form for the number 5,320,080?
    a. five million, thirty-two thousand, eighty
    b. five million, three hundred twenty thousand, eighty
    c. five million, three hundred twenty thousand, eight
    d. five thousand, three hundred twenty-eight

19. Round 514,684.51 to the thousands place.
    a. 510,000.00
    b. 514,000.00
    c. 515,000.00
    d. 520,000.00

20. A large rectangular-prism-shaped tank at the zoo is 8 feet wide and 5 feet high. How long is the tank if it holds a volume of 200 cubic feet of water?
    a. 5 feet
    b. 6 feet
    c. 8 feet
    d. 13 feet

21. Mr. Aguilera needs 71 feet of fencing that costs $3.98 per foot. Which is the best approximation for the price of the fencing?
    a. $210
    b. $240
    c. $280
    d. $320

22. A ship is located on the map at coordinates (4, 9). If the radar indicates the lighthouse is 5 units east and 4 units south of the ship, what is the location of the lighthouse?

North

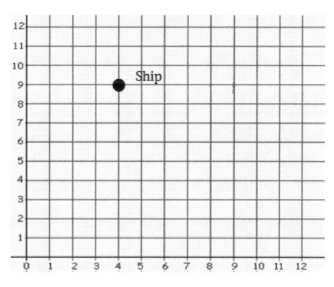

South

   a. (9, 5)
   b. (9, 4)
   c. (8, 3)
   d. (9, 13)

23. The side length of a regular pentagon is 6.5 centimeters. What is the perimeter of this figure?
   a. 26.0 cm
   b. 32.5 cm
   c. 39.0 cm
   d. 42.25 cm

6.5
$\times \underline{5}$

24. The length of the football field near Gerald's school is 120 yards. What is the length of the field in feet?
   a. 12 feet
   b. 360 feet
   c. 400 feet
   d. 1,440 feet

- 75 -

25. Evan measured the amount of rain in the gauge over the weekend. On Saturday, he measured $1\frac{6}{10}$ inches and on Sunday, $\frac{8}{10}$ inches. What is the total amount of rain, in inches, Evan measured on those two days, written in the simplest form?

    a. $1\frac{2}{5}$

    b. $1\frac{4}{10}$

    c. $1\frac{14}{20}$

    d. $2\frac{2}{5}$

26. Given the isosceles trapezoid PQRS below, which two sides are congruent?

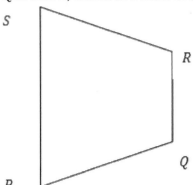

    a. $\overline{PS}$ and $\overline{QR}$
    b. $\overline{RS}$ and $\overline{QP}$
    c. $\overline{QP}$ and $\overline{RQ}$
    d. $\overline{PS}$ and $\overline{RS}$

27. William needs to find the value of the expression below. What is the value of this expression?

        $40 - 4(3 - 1)$
    a. 29
    b. 32
    c. 72
    d. 107

28. Annette read that out of 20 televisions sold in her state last year, 3 were Brand V. If a furniture store near her home sold 360 televisions last year, about how many should Annette expect to be Brand V?

    a. 18
    b. 54
    c. 1,080
    d. 2,400

29. Curtis measured the temperature of water in a flask in Science class. The temperature of the water was 35°C. He carefully heated the flask so that the temperature of the water increased about 2°C every 3 minutes. Approximately how much had the temperature of the water increased after 20 minutes?

    a. 10°C
    b. 13°C
    c. 15°C
    d. 35°C

30. Express the calculation "subtract 4 from 18, then divide by 7."

    a. $(4 - 18) \div 7$
    b. $4 - 18 \div 7$
    c. $(18 - 4) \div 7$
    d. $18 - 4 \div 7$

Section 5 – Essay

Write an essay on the following prompt on the paper provided. Your essay should NOT exceed 2 pages and must be written in blue or black ink. You are not allowed to use scrap paper, a dictionary, or a thesaurus.

Prompt: <u>Should public schools be allowed to sell junk food such as chips and soda?</u>

Support your position with specific examples from personal experience, the experience of others, current events, history, or literature.

Answers and Explanations

Section 1: Verbal Reasoning

1. D: A teacher provides instruction and information to an individual or group of individuals. An instructor functions in the same capacity, that is, in the practice of teaching.

2. C: To say something was done instantly means that it was done immediately and without hesitation.

3. B: Something that is described as gigantic is extremely large, or huge, in size.

4. C: Something that is costly is expensive because it costs a lot of money.

5. D: To say that something is done frequently implies that it is done regularly or often.

6. D: Something that is being observed is being watched. Binoculars are used to see things more clearly, so it makes sense that the man would be observing or watching eagles with binoculars.

7. B: Saying that somebody purchased something and saying they bought something conveys the same meaning.

8. D: When it is said that something is entire, it usually means that it is still whole. For example, if someone says they ate an entire apple, it is the same as saying they ate a whole apple.

9. A: To say something is superior to something else usually implies that it is better.

10. A: When a selection is being made, it involves making a choice between several options. Selecting something is the same as choosing something.

11. B: When something is done swiftly, it means that it is done fast or quickly.

12. D: Chuckled is a synonym for laughed. To say somebody chuckled or to say that somebody laughed conveys the same meaning.

13. C: To locate something that is lost or misplaced is to find it. For example, the child could not locate (find) his toy.

14. B: If somebody is puzzled about something, it implies confusion or bewilderment. For example, to say that a man was puzzled by the woman's reaction means that the man was confused by her reaction.

15. D: Something that is cheap does not cost a substantial amount of money. Saying something is cheap and saying that something is inexpensive conveys the same meaning.

16. D: When somebody is described as intelligent, it usually means that they are smart.

17. A: Something that is required is needed. For example, if you say you require ten dollars to buy lunch, it implies that you need ten dollars for lunch.

18. A: Humiliated means embarrassment or hurting someone's self-respect. Since the star is wearing a disguise, it is unlikely that the star fears being overlooked (C) or ignored (B). Instead, the star does not want to get their attention. The evasive tactics are to avoid being noticed or humiliated by their attention. Being welcomed (D) carries a positive connotation and is thus less likely to be avoided.

19. D: A fashion expert's identifying something as out-of-date would be negative, not a compliment. So, the expert would not applaud Sylvia's clothing (A) or praise her accessories (C), which both have positive connotations. The verb drafted (B) means that someone or something is chosen from a group. Drafting can also refer to someone who has started to write a paper or started to put together a plan.

20. A: The others were acquainted with—i.e., knew about or were familiar with—Steve's strange behavior and thus were not upset by it. Appalled (B) and disgusted (C) are synonyms meaning that they certainly were upset with the behavior. However, this would contradict the sentence's statement that they were not upset. Unfamiliar (D) is an antonym of acquainted. While unfamiliarity with some things could prevent someone from being upset about them, this sentence describes Steve's behavior as strange, which is more likely to upset people who are unfamiliar with it than those who are used to it.

21. A: The description of "poor little" Ike implies that Ned's handling of the hose caused something unfortunate and unintended to happen to Ike, like being drenched with water, which could be caused by clumsy handling. So, the context of the sentence does not suggest that Ike was entertained (C). If the handling of the hose was clumsy, then this would not cause Ike to stay dry (B) because it does not explain why he is "poor little" Ike. Again, the context of the sentence does suggest that Ike was unaffected (D) because nothing good seems to have happened to Ike.

22. B: Expressly means specifically, particularly, especially, precisely, exactly. Generally (C) and commonly (A) are antonyms of expressly. Possibly (D), meaning not definitely/not surely, is also an antonym of expressly, precisely, exactly.

23. D: Starved means very hungry. So, if James is famished, he could eat an immense, i.e., very large, meal. Nauseated (B) means sick. So, if James were not well, he could not eat an immense meal. Congested (A) means overly full or stuffed. If James exclaimed that he was congested, he probably would not be interested in any kind of meal. Also, if James were satisfied (C), then he would obviously not be interested in a meal.

24. A: Collected means gather, group, or accumulate. The context of the sentence tells us that the student does not want to be a distraction. So, the student would not hoist (D) (i.e., raise or lift) his things into the air before leaving the classroom. Discipline (C) means to instruct or to order and is reserved for people or animals, not things like classroom materials. Choice B is not the correct choice because the word delay suggests being late and classroom materials cannot be late.

25. B: Instantaneous means immediate, in an instant, right away. To discount her means to dismiss or ignore. Illegible (A) means that someone's writing or print is very difficult to read or understand. Luscious (C) means that something is delicious or sweet which does not make sense in this

sentence. Unpredictable (D) means changeable, erratic, unreliable, and unforeseeable and could be an adjective with "his reaction." However, to discount her for lying is a predictable reaction.

26. B: Clever means brilliant, perceptive, able, and skilled. Since the method the inventor found resolved his product's design problem, it is logical that it was clever. Ingenuous (D) means honest, trusting, and sincere. Incompetent (C) and awkward (A) mean unskillful or inadequate and are antonyms of clever.

27. D: Refused means not allowed, rejected, denied. Gainful means profitable, productive, lucrative, money-making. If Glenda has gainful employment, she will be denied disability benefits, which are given to applicants who are disabled from any gainful employment. So Glenda would not be granted (C), given (B), or assigned (A) disability benefits for having employment.

28. C: To irritate means to annoy, aggravate, or upset. Since the sentence begins with a warning and since the student behavior of talking during lectures is generally an unpopular one with teachers, this choice fits best in the sentence. To delight (B), or please, to aid (A), or help, and to soothe (D), or calm, are all opposites of irritate, hence do not fit the sentence meaning.

29. A: Anxieties are worries, fears, doubts, and apprehensions. Delicious is an adjective that can describe a meal and later digestive problems certainly can be worthy of anxieties. Diffuse (B) as a verb means that something is spread out which does not fit the context of this sentence. When someone or something is enshrined (C), the person or object is marked as important and should not be harmed. So, this does not fit the context of the sentence. An antonym of anxieties is hopes (D) which is very unlikely for someone in this situation.

30. B: A blizzard is a snow storm that lasts for several hours with high winds and freezing temperatures. So, this kind of storm would delay a journey for people who wanted to camp during the winter. The campers are not auditioning (A) (i.e., a try out or interview) for a position. Also, the campers would not be concerned about a mortgage (C) (i.e., a type of loan that people use to purchase a house). Suffrage (D) is the right to vote which would not be concern for campers facing a blizzard.

31. B: The adverb shamelessly means that someone shows no regret or sadness about a wrong action. To manipulate someone is to use, control, maneuver, deceive, take advantage of that person. The action of manipulating a child is one that should be seen as intolerable which means unacceptable. Also, the witness of the event clearly thinks that this is not acceptable behavior by calling it shameless. So, the witness would not think of it as admirable (A) which means excellent or respectful. A maternal (C) action is one that is kind, protective, and reminds others of good mothers. However, this is not the case for a shameless action on a child. Finally, prodigal (D) is an adjective that describes a foolish waste of time or money. So, this does not fit the context of this sentence.

32. B: Conflicting means opposing or clashing, so feeling discomfort would be a conflicting effect of a medication. Beneficial (A) is an antonym of conflicting and refers to that which is positive, favorable, helpful. Desirable (C) means wanted or healthful, a synonym of beneficial, as is useful (D). These are all positive adjectives and are inconsistent with the negative effect of feeling discomfort.

33. B: A deceitful person says one thing but does another. The word carries a negative connotation that is consistent with an accusation, i.e., a charge of wrongdoing. Accusations would be "happily" proven false. Accusations are not made about a hero (C), who is a positive figure. Also, a public figure would not happily want claims of heroism to be proven false. Accusations do not fit someone

who is commendable (A), meaning someone who is respected or worthy of praise. Calling someone a commendable person would not be "happily" proven false. Again, a pleasant (D) man is someone who is kind and gentle. These admirable qualities would want to be proven true.

34. B: A disinterested third party is one that is detached or uninvolved in the work mentioned. Prejudiced (C), literally meaning prejudging, without knowledge or basis, is an antonym of disinterested. Revolutionary (D), meaning radical or rebellious does not fit the context of the sentence. After all, a rebellious and radical person may not be the best person to give disinterested feedback. Biased (A), meaning slanted, inclined, distorted, is an antonym of disinterested.

Section 2: Quantitative Reasoning

1. D: The perimeter (P) of the quadrilateral is simply the sum of its sides:
$P = m + (m + 2) + (m + 3) + 2m$
Put together like terms by adding the variables (m terms) together. Then, add the constants. This gives you: $P = 5m + 5$
In this problem, it seems that some of the variables do not have a number in front of them. However, when there is no coefficient, this means multiplication by 1. So, $m = 1m$, $x = 1x$, and so on.

2. D: Since the probability of being born in the spring or summer is being calculated, the probabilities are added. $\frac{7}{20} + \frac{3}{20} = \frac{10}{20} = \frac{1}{2}$.

3. C: A diagram of the plot would look like this:

W=8m

L=3W=24m

The perimeter of a rectangle is the formula $P = 2L + 2W$ which produces $2(24) + 2(8) = 48 + 16 = 64\ m$.

4. D: To find the volume of the rectangular prism, find the number of cubes in the figure. The figure has two layers of cubes. On the top layer, the number of cubes can be counted. There are 12 cubes on the top layer. The bottom layer is the same as the top, so there are also 12 cubes in the bottom layer. There are 24 total cubes in the figure, so the volume of the figure is 24 units[3].

5. B: The value of y is indeed 4 times the value of x. Note. 4 is 4 times the value of 1; 8 is 4 times the value of 2; 12 is 4 times the value of 3; and 16 is 4 times the value of 4.

6. A: $C \div S$. Since the cookies are being divided up equally between the S students. Use some numbers to help see the correct answer. If $C = 40$ and $S = 10$.
$\qquad C \div S = 40 \div 10 = 4$

The incorrect choices produce the following with these values:
$$C \times S = 40 \times 10 = 400$$
$$C - S = 40 - 10 = 30$$
$$S \div C = 10 \div 40 = \frac{1}{4}$$
None of these seem reasonable.

7. D: Since Harlan knows the cost of each bag of carrots, and also how many total carrots he needs, he also needs to know the number of carrots in each bag to find the number of bags he needs to buy. Then, he can multiply the number of bags by the price to find the amount of money the carrots for his stew will cost.

8. A: To solve, test each answer. Notice that in (A), the numerator has been multiplied by 3 to get 12. The denominator has been multiplied by 3 to get 21. In (B) the numerator has been multiplied by 4 and the denominator has been multiplied by 5. In (C), the numerator has been multiplied by 3 and the denominator has been multiplied by 4. In (D), the numerator has been multiplied by 4 and the denominator has been multiplied by a number less than 4.

9. C: Aaron ran four miles from home and then back again, so he ran a total of eight miles. Therefore, statement III is false. Statements I and II, however, are both true. Since Aaron ran eight miles in eighty minutes, he ran an average of one mile every ten minutes, or six miles per hour; he ran two miles from point A to B in 20 minutes and four miles from D to E in 40 minutes, so his running speed between both sets of points was the same.

10. B: The total number of Evercell batteries is $(4 \times E)$ and the total number of Durapower batteries is $(6 \times D)$. The sum of the two is the total number of batteries in the store.

11. A: To solve, first figure out how much room is left when her car and the garage are taken into account: 19 feet – 15 feet = 4 feet. To center the car, it would have to be parked 2 feet from the front of the garage.

12. C: Notice that Set M starts with 1 and increases by adding 3 each time, so the numbers more than 20 in this set are: (22, 25, 28, 31, …) Set V is the set of odd numbers, so the numbers in this set greater than 20 are: (21, 23, 25, 27, 29, …) The first number common to both sets is 25.

13. D: To solve, isolate the x on one side of the equation.
4x = 36 – 4
4x = 32
x = 8

14. A: $C = \frac{3}{4}(100) + 20$. Since $\frac{1}{4}$ of the original $100 was sent to the savings account, $\frac{3}{4}$ of the money was kept in cash. The bonus was then added afterward.

15. C: The scalene triangle does not have a line of symmetry. The hexagon has two lines of symmetry, the arrow as one line of symmetry and the curve has one line of symmetry.

16. D: There are perpendicular edges at every corner of the cube.

17. C: The fraction of Figure A that is shaded is $\frac{2}{5}$. The fraction of Figure B that is shaded is $\frac{12}{30}$. $\frac{12}{30}$ reduces to $\frac{2}{5}$ by dividing the numerator and denominator by 6. Therefore, fractions of the shaded regions are equal.

18. B: The situation may be modeled with the equation $\frac{1}{3} + \frac{1}{2} = \frac{1}{t}$, which simplifies to $\frac{5}{6} = \frac{1}{t}$. Thus, $t = \frac{6}{5}$. If working together, it will take them 1.2 hours to decorate the cake.

19. A: The simplest way to compare the two pieces of pie is to find a common dominator for both fractions. The older daughter was given 2/5 of the pie, while the younger daughter was given 1/3 of the pie. The least common dominator for the two fractions is 15. Therefore, the older daughter received 6/15 of the pie and the younger daughter received 5/15 of the pie. 6/15 is larger than 5/15; therefore, the older daughter received a larger slice of the pie.

20. C: Since one half of the wealth is being distributed in 5 equal parts, each relative is receiving $\frac{1}{5}$ of the $\frac{1}{2}$. In other words $\frac{1}{5} \times \frac{1}{2} = \frac{1}{10}$.

21. B: Since 3 items are being purchased and each costs $3.99, these two numbers must be multiplied. Choice A shows $3 \times 4 - 3 \times 0.01 = 3 \times (4 - 0.01) = 3 \times 3.99$. Choice C shows $3 \times 3 + 3 \times 0.9 + 3 \times 0.09 = 3 \times (3 + 0.9 + 0.09) = 3 \times 3.99$. Choice D shows $3.99 + 3.99 + 3.99 = 3 \times 3.99$. Only choice B shows a different operation: division.

22. D: A line of symmetry is a line where the figure could be folded in half to match up perfectly with itself. Each one of the lines is a line of symmetry because each point on one side of the figure is the same distance from the line of symmetry, and the line segment that can be created by connecting each point with its corresponding point will be perpendicular to the line of symmetry.

23. B: Choice A is a number in the thousandths; D is a number in the hundredths; C and B are in tenths. Four-tenths is the largest of these choices.

24. B: The formula for the area of trapezoids is not necessarily needed here to do this problem. Since the relationship between the area, A, and the height, h, can be seen in the chart, looking at the third and fourth columns to see if there is a pattern will show a relationship between the variables. Each value in the area column is equal to 6 times the value in the height column. So, we get $A = 6h$.

25. A: By adding all of the dimes, we find that there are a total of 100 dimes in the bag. 10 of them were minted in 1945. The probability, then, of choosing a dime minted in 1945 is 10 out of 100, which is equivalent to the fraction $\frac{1}{10}$.

26. D: This procedure first finds the area to be fertilized, by multiplying the length and width of the rectangular yard. Then, it divides that area by the area each pound of fertilizer will cover.

27. C: To answer this question correctly, convert all numbers to decimal form to make them easy to compare. Since two of the numbers are already in decimal form, we only need to convert $1\frac{7}{10}$ and $1\frac{3}{4}$ to decimal form.

$$7 \div 10 = 0.7, \text{ so } 1\frac{7}{10} = 1.7$$
$$\text{and } 3 \div 4 = 0.75, \text{ so } 1\frac{3}{4} = 1.75$$

Therefore, by comparing place values from left to right of 1.7, 1.72, 1.75 and 1.695, we see that 1.695 is least, 1.7 is next greatest, 1.72 is next, and 1.75 is greatest. So, Antonio should buy the border that is $1\frac{3}{4}$ inches wide.

28. D: Only answer D correctly shows each amount of salt being subtracted from the original total amount of 26 ounces that was in the box.

29. A: The box symbol shown at $\angle R$ means that $\angle R$ measures 90°. Since we are told $m\angle S$ is 20° less than $m\angle R$, subtract 90 –20 to get 70. This means that $m\angle S = 70°$. The sum of $m\angle R$ and $m\angle S$ is found by adding: 90 +70 = 160. The sum of all angles in a triangle always adds up to 180°, so subtracting 180 – 160 results in a difference of 20. So, $m\angle T$ is 20°.

30. B: To answer this question, that there are 9 equal-sized panes in the window. Of the 9 panes, 3 have a dark tint and can be represented by the fraction, $\frac{3}{9}$, which is equivalent to $\frac{1}{3}$. 2 of the panes are lightly tinted and can be represented by $\frac{2}{9}$. So, the number sentence, $\frac{1}{3} + \frac{2}{9} = \frac{5}{9}$ best represents the total section of the window which is tinted.

31. B: If each car brought from 1 to 3 people, then 50 is the best estimate of the number of people that could have arrived in the 25 cars. 25 is too low because this would mean only 1 person could have arrived in each car. 75 and 100 are too high, because then this would mean 3 or more people arrived in each car. The answer, 50 people, would mean that each car brought 2 people each, which is the average number of people who arrived per car.

32. D: Note that the ratio asked for is the number of people who ordered milk to the number who ordered juice. The number of people who ordered coffee does not matter here. This compares 10 to 25, and the order is important here. Since the ratio is with the number of people who ordered milk first, the 10 must come first. So, the ratio is 10 to 25, but the ratio can be written in simpler form by dividing both numbers in the ratio by 5, to get the ratio: 2 to 5.

33. C: Looking at the chart, a pattern can be seen in the relationship between the number of gills and the number of fluid ounces. Each number of gills in the first column, when multiplied by 4, gives the number of fluid ounces in the second column. So, f equals 4 times g, or $f = 4g$.

34. D: The amount charged for miles hauled will require us to multiply the number of miles by $0.05. The charge for each load of $80 is not changed by the number of miles hauled. That will be added to the amount charged for miles hauled. So, the equation needs to show 0.05 times miles plus 80, or $c = 0.05m + 80$.

35. B: A cube has six square faces. The arrangement of these faces in a two-dimensional figure is a net of a cube if the figure can be folded to form a cube. Figures A, C, and D represent three of the eleven possible nets of a cube. If choice B is folded, however, the bottom square in the second

column will overlap the fourth square in the top row, so the figure does not represent a net of a cube.

36. B: A right angle has a measure of 90 degrees, which is greater than the measure of an acute angle, with an angle less than 90 degrees. A right angle also has a measure less than the measure of an obtuse angle, which has a measure greater than 90 degrees.

37. C: The pattern in the table is that the number of customers is increasing by 25 each week. This means that there should be $205 + 25 = 230$ customers expected in week 4.

Week	Customers
1	155
2	180
3	205
4	230

+25
+25
+25

38. D: There are 12 even-numbered floors between floors 1 and 25. At each one, the elevator gains 2 people, for a net gain of 24. There are 11 odd-numbered floors between floors 1 and 25 (not counting floors 1 and 25). At each one, the elevator loses 1 person, for a net loss of 11. The elevator leaves the first floor with 3 people, so the total arriving at the 25th floor is 3 + 24 – 11 = 16.

Section 3: Reading Comprehension

1. A: If someone is "elated", they are extremely happy and excited about something.

2. D: The first sentence of paragraph 3 uses a simile when it says Scott "stood like a statue." A simile uses "like" or "as" to compare one thing to another.

3. B: Choice B most clearly and completely expresses the theme of the story. Coach Travis tells Scott that "it's all about perspective", and then says that how Scott decides to look at it is up to him.

4. C: Choice C is the most complete and accurate summary of the story overall. A, B, and D are incorrect because they cover only part of the story or some of the main ideas and concepts.

5. A: Scott is upset in the story because he feels responsible for the team's loss.

6. B: is the best choice because the main purpose of dance in Native American culture is to communicate a message. A, C, and D are not the best choices because they do not accurately reflect the main purpose of dance in Native American culture.

7. A: is the best choice because the Iroquois corn husk dance and the Hopi Snake Ceremonial were both intended to bring good crops. B, C, and D are not the best choices because they do not represent the purpose of these dances.

8. D: is the best choice because it is the only statement of fact. A, B, and C are not the best choices because they are all statements of opinion.

9. C: is the best choice because in many Native American tribes the eagle feather represents strength. A, B, and D are not the best choices because they do not reflect the meaning of the eagle feather in many Native American tribes.

10. A: is the best choice because the author's main purpose in writing this article is to inform the reader. B, C, and D are not the best choices because the author's primary purpose in writing this article is not to entertain, to influence, or to persuade.

11. B: You may already know that a conifer is a type of tree. If you do not know this, you can deduce the information based on the fact that the word is used in the description of the Giant Sequoia tree.

12. D: In the first sentence, the passage states that *most* people think the Giant Sequoia is the largest organism. It goes on to explain that there are some people who do not agree.

13. C: The first paragraph describes the General Sherman as the largest Giant Sequoia. The other answer choices include words that can be found in the passage

14. C: Look at lines 10 - 12 to find the answer. The passage explains that goldenrod flowers and aspen groves are connected with underground root systems, leading some people to believe that these organisms are bigger than Giant Sequoia trees.

15. D: The passage gives the diameter of the tree at the bottom, but the diameter at the top is not given. You cannot assume the answer, so there is no way to know what the diameter is given the data in the passage.

16. C: is the best choice because the official name of the Alamo is San Antonio de Valero. A, B, and D are not the best choices because they list incorrect official names for the Alamo.

17. A: is the best choice because the author's purpose in writing "Remember the Alamo" is clearly to inform. B, C, and D are not the best choices because they represent inaccurate purposes for the story.

18. D: is the best choice because freedom was the main motivation for those who fought at the Alamo. A, B, and C are not the best choices because they do not portray the primary motivation for the Alamo fighters.

19. B: is the best choice because the Alamo was designed to serve many purposes in the community. A, C, and D are not the best choices because they do not reflect the real purpose behind the design of the Alamo.

20. D: is the best choice because it is a statement of opinion. A, B, and C are not the best choices because they are all statements of fact.

21. B: The passage gives general instructions for tomato plant culture from seeding to providing support for the vines. Answers A and D are too specific, focusing on details of the text. Answer C is too general: the passage does not fully describe how to operate a farm.

22. C: The passage states that seeds germinated in late March will be ready for the garden after the last frost.

23. A: The passage states that seeds germinated in late March will be ready for the garden after the last frost, implying that exposure to freezing temperatures would harm them.

24. A: The text states that pinching the bud is done to make the plants stronger.

25. D: Although all the other answers make mention of information contained in the paragraph, the overall purpose of this paragraph is as stated, to describe the support procedure.

Section 4: Mathematics Achievement

1. C: Add the 1 hour and 30 minutes to find that Janice finishes her homework at 4:15 PM. Next, add 1 hour and 45 minutes to find that Janice returns home at 6:00 PM.

2. A: The digit 5 is in the 5th column, which is the ten thousands column. Therefore the digit represents the value 50,000.

3. C: The value of each number in the pattern is a multiple of 100. Therefore, the 14th number represents the value of the product of 14 and 100; $14 \times 100 = 1400$.

4. D: The recipe is being multiplied by 4 in this problem, therefore $\frac{1}{8} = \frac{4}{32}$ so a total of 4 cups of milk are needed. Since this is not one of the choices, a conversion is needed. 1 pint = 2 cups and 1 quart = 2 pints, therefore 1 quart = 4 cups.

5. C: This is a simple subtraction problem involving money. $25 -$18 = $7

6. A: To find the difference, subtract. It is important to align decimal places. Note, when subtracting here, the digit in the hundredths place in 0.33 has no digit aligned above it. We must add a zero to 1.5 so that we can align the hundredths places correctly. Now we can subtract 33 hundredths from the 50 hundredths to get 17 hundredths. So, we get 1.17 as our correct answer.

7. C: This is a simple addition problem. Line up the decimals so that they are all in the same place in the equation, and see that there is a 3 by itself in the hundredths column. Then add the tenths column: 6+3+5 to get 14. Write down the 4 and carry the 1. Add the ones column: 3 plus the carried 1. Write down 4. Then write down the 1.

8. A: Multiply 24 by 4 to get 96 and multiply 12 by 6 to get 72. Then, add 96 and 72 to get the correct answer, 168.

9. C: To solve this formula, follow the order of operations. First, add what is in the parenthesis, 4 + 2, to get 6. Then, multiply the 6 by 35 to get 210. Last, we should add 20 + 210 + 47 to get 277.

10. B: Write 606, then add the decimal in the thousandths place, the third place from the right.

11. B: There are 2 green sections on the spinner and the spinner has 6 sections in all. The probability of spinning green is 2 out of 6, when expressed as a fraction is $\frac{2}{6}$. Written in simplest terms, the fraction is $\frac{1}{3}$.

12. C: The number line is divided into tenths. Thus, between the whole numbers, 5 and 6, lie the decimals, 5.1, 5.2, 5.3, 5.4, 5.5, 5.6, 5.7, 5.8, and 5.9. Point P represents the decimal, 5.8.

13. B: By changing the mixed numbers into improper fractions, $4\frac{1}{3} - 2\frac{2}{3}$ becomes $\frac{13}{3} - \frac{8}{3} = \frac{5}{3}$. Changing $\frac{5}{3}$ back into a mixed number yields $1\frac{2}{3}$.

14. D: The mean is just the average. To calculate this, find the total of all 10 numbers by adding. Then, divide that total by 10 because that is the number of data points. The total is 750, so the mean of this group of numbers is 75.

15. B: To answer this question, find the total number of bulbs required by multiplying 10 by 3. The number of packages of bulbs required can be found by dividing this total number of bulbs, 30, by 5, to find that 6 packages are needed. Then, multiplying 6 by the cost per package, 8, we find that the total cost for all the bulbs needed was $48.

16. C: First, find the least common denominator: $\frac{4\times16}{5\times16} - \frac{1\times5}{16\times5} = \frac{64}{80} - \frac{5}{80}$, then subtract the numerators: $\frac{64}{80} - \frac{5}{80} = \frac{59}{80}$. To find where this answer lies on the number line, consider that $0 = \frac{0}{80}, \frac{1}{4} = \frac{20}{80}, \frac{1}{2} = \frac{40}{80}, \frac{3}{4} = \frac{60}{80},$ and $1 = \frac{80}{80}$. So $\frac{59}{80}$ is between $\frac{40}{80} = \frac{1}{2}$ and $\frac{60}{80} = \frac{3}{4}$.

17. C: The right triangle is being rotated 90 degrees in a clockwise direction about the vertex point (2, 5).

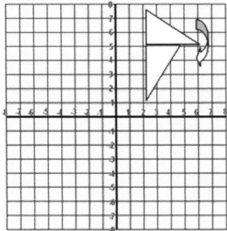

18. B: The value of A is 5,032,080; the value of C is 5,320,008; and the value of D is 5,328. B shows 5,320,080 which is the original number.

19. C: To round to the thousands place, look at the digit to the right (in the hundreds place). If that digit is 4 or less, leave the digit in the thousands place; if that digit is 5 or more, add one to the digit in the thousands place.

20. A: Use the volume of a rectangular prism formula $V = L \times W \times H$ to determine the length of the tank.
$$200 = L \times 8 \times 5 \rightarrow 200 = 40L \rightarrow L = 5 \text{ feet.}$$

21. C: The approximate price of the fence is found by rounding to 70 feet at \$4 per foot. $P = 70 \times \$4 = \$280$. The actual price is $P = 71 \times \$3.98 = \$282.58$.

22. A.: Translate the point 5 units to the right and 4 units down to find the location of the lighthouse.

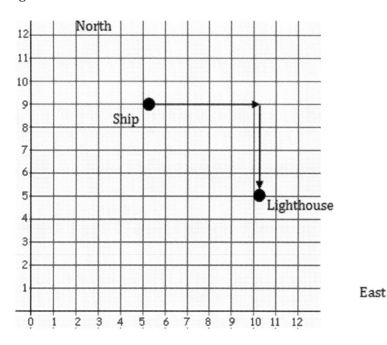

23. B: A regular pentagon is a 5 sided figure with all sides equal in length. Therefore the perimeter is $5 \times 6.5 = 32.5$ centimeters.

24. B: There are 3 feet in every yard. Since we are converting from a larger unit to a smaller unit, we should multiply the number of the larger unit by the conversion factor. That is 120 times 3 equals 360.

25. D: To answer this question, note that the fractions have common denominators. When adding fractions with common denominators, we need to add only the numerators, so, the sum of $\frac{6}{10}$ and $\frac{8}{10}$ is $\frac{14}{10}$. This should then be written as a mixed number, $1\frac{4}{10}$, which is found by dividing 14 by 10 which gives the whole number and the remainder becomes your new numerator over the same denominator of 10. The fraction $\frac{4}{10}$ can also be written as $\frac{2}{5}$ by dividing numerator and denominator by the common factor of 2. Therefore, $\frac{14}{10}$ is equivalent

to $1\frac{2}{5}$. Be careful here to remember the 1 from the original $1\frac{6}{10}$ amount given in the problem, which must be added to the $1\frac{2}{5}$ to make a total of $2\frac{2}{5}$.

26. B: By the definition of an isosceles trapezoid, the legs (non-parallel sides) are congruent. Since the figure is defined as an isosceles, it is known that $\overline{PS}$ and $\overline{QR}$ are parallel and not congruent in length.

27. B: To simplify this expression, use the order of operations. First, do what is in the parenthesis and subtract 1 from 3 to get 2. Then, we multiply 4 times 2 to get 8. Last, subtract the 8 from 40 to get 32.

28. B: One method that can be used to answer this question is to write and solve the proportion: $\frac{3}{20} = \frac{V}{360}$, where V stands for the number of Brand V televisions that were sold at the furniture store. To solve the proportion, we can cross multiply: 20 times V and 3 times 360, which gives the equation: $20V = 1{,}080$. We solve this equation by dividing both sides of the equation by 20 to get $V = 54$.

29. B: The water temperature increased by about 2° every 3 minutes, or $\frac{2}{3}$ of a degree every minute. Multiplying the increase in degrees per minute by the total number of minutes yields

$$\frac{2°}{3 \text{ min}} \times 20 \text{ min} = \frac{40}{3}, \text{ or } 13.33°$$

Since the problem asks for the increase in temperature and not the total temperature that results after the increases, 13 is the closest to our answer.

30. C: When subtraction comes before division, it must be placed in parentheses. The phrase "subtract 4 from 18" means the same as "18 minus 4."

Secret Key #1 - Time is Your Greatest Enemy

Pace Yourself

Wear a watch. At the beginning of the test, check the time (or start a chronometer on your watch to count the minutes), and check the time after every few questions to make sure you are "on schedule."

If you are forced to speed up, do it efficiently. Usually one or more answer choices can be eliminated without too much difficulty. Above all, don't panic. Don't speed up and just begin guessing at random choices. By pacing yourself, and continually monitoring your progress against your watch, you will always know exactly how far ahead or behind you are with your available time. If you find that you are one minute behind on the test, don't skip one question without spending any time on it, just to catch back up. Take 15 fewer seconds on the next four questions, and after four questions you'll have caught back up. Once you catch back up, you can continue working each problem at your normal pace.

Furthermore, don't dwell on the problems that you were rushed on. If a problem was taking up too much time and you made a hurried guess, it must be difficult. The difficult questions are the ones you are most likely to miss anyway, so it isn't a big loss. It is better to end with more time than you need than to run out of time.

Lastly, sometimes it is beneficial to slow down if you are constantly getting ahead of time. You are always more likely to catch a careless mistake by working more slowly than quickly, and among very high-scoring test takers (those who are likely to have lots of time left over), careless errors affect the score more than mastery of material.

Secret Key #2 - Guessing is not Guesswork

You probably know that guessing is a good idea. Unlike other standardized tests, there is no penalty for getting a wrong answer. Even if you have no idea about a question, you still have a 20-25% chance of getting it right.

Most test takers do not understand the impact that proper guessing can have on their score. Unless you score extremely high, guessing will significantly contribute to your final score.

Monkeys Take the Test

What most test takers don't realize is that to insure that 20-25% chance, you have to guess randomly. If you put 20 monkeys in a room to take this test, assuming they answered once per question and behaved themselves, on average they would get 20-25% of the questions correct. Put 20 test takers in the room, and the average will be much lower among guessed questions. Why?

1. The test writers intentionally write deceptive answer choices that "look" right. A test taker has no idea about a question, so he picks the "best looking" answer, which is often wrong. The monkey has no idea what looks good and what doesn't, so it will consistently be right about 20-25% of the time.
2. Test takers will eliminate answer choices from the guessing pool based on a hunch or intuition. Simple but correct answers often get excluded, leaving a 0% chance of being correct. The monkey has no clue, and often gets lucky with the best choice.

This is why the process of elimination endorsed by most test courses is flawed and detrimental to your performance. Test takers don't guess; they make an ignorant stab in the dark that is usually worse than random.

$5 Challenge

Let me introduce one of the most valuable ideas of this course—the $5 challenge:

You only mark your "best guess" if you are willing to bet $5 on it.
You only eliminate choices from guessing if you are willing to bet $5 on it.

Why $5? Five dollars is an amount of money that is small yet not insignificant, and can really add up fast (20 questions could cost you $100). Likewise, each answer choice on one question of the test will have a small impact on your overall score, but it can really add up to a lot of points in the end.

The process of elimination IS valuable. The following shows your chance of guessing it right:

If you eliminate wrong answer choices until only this many remain:	Chance of getting it correct:
1	100%
2	50%
3	33%

However, if you accidentally eliminate the right answer or go on a hunch for an incorrect answer, your chances drop dramatically—to 0%. By guessing among all the answer choices, you are GUARANTEED to have a shot at the right answer.

That's why the $5 test is so valuable. If you give up the advantage and safety of a pure guess, it had better be worth the risk.

What we still haven't covered is how to be sure that whatever guess you make is truly random. Here's the easiest way:

Always pick the first answer choice among those remaining.

Such a technique means that you have decided, **before you see a single test question**, exactly how you are going to guess, and since the order of choices tells you nothing about which one is correct, this guessing technique is perfectly random.

This section is not meant to scare you away from making educated guesses or eliminating choices; you just need to define when a choice is worth eliminating. The $5 test, along with a pre-defined random guessing strategy, is the best way to make sure you reap all of the benefits of guessing.

Secret Key #3 - Practice Smarter, Not Harder

Many test takers delay the test preparation process because they dread the awful amounts of practice time they think necessary to succeed on the test. We have refined an effective method that will take you only a fraction of the time.

There are a number of "obstacles" in the path to success. Among these are answering questions, finishing in time, and mastering test-taking strategies. All must be executed on the day of the test at peak performance, or your score will suffer. The test is a mental marathon that has a large impact on your future.

Just like a marathon runner, it is important to work your way up to the full challenge. So first you just worry about questions, and then time, and finally strategy:

Success Strategy

1. Find a good source for practice tests.
2. If you are willing to make a larger time investment, consider using more than one study guide. Often the different approaches of multiple authors will help you "get" difficult concepts.
3. Take a practice test with no time constraints, with all study helps, "open book." Take your time with questions and focus on applying strategies.
4. Take a practice test with time constraints, with all guides, "open book."
5. Take a final practice test without open material and with time limits.

If you have time to take more practice tests, just repeat step 5. By gradually exposing yourself to the full rigors of the test environment, you will condition your mind to the stress of test day and maximize your success.

Secret Key #4 - Prepare, Don't Procrastinate

Let me state an obvious fact: if you take the test three times, you will probably get three different scores. This is due to the way you feel on test day, the level of preparedness you have, and the version of the test you see. Despite the test writers' claims to the contrary, some versions of the test WILL be easier for you than others.

Since your future depends so much on your score, you should maximize your chances of success. In order to maximize the likelihood of success, you've got to prepare in advance. This means taking practice tests and spending time learning the information and test taking strategies you will need to succeed.

Never go take the actual test as a "practice" test, expecting that you can just take it again if you need to. Take all the practice tests you can on your own, but when you go to take the official test, be prepared, be focused, and do your best the first time!

Secret Key #5 - Test Yourself

Everyone knows that time is money. There is no need to spend too much of your time or too little of your time preparing for the test. You should only spend as much of your precious time preparing as is necessary for you to get the score you need.

Once you have taken a practice test under real conditions of time constraints, then you will know if you are ready for the test or not.

If you have scored extremely high the first time that you take the practice test, then there is not much point in spending countless hours studying. You are already there.

Benchmark your abilities by retaking practice tests and seeing how much you have improved. Once you consistently score high enough to guarantee success, then you are ready.

If you have scored well below where you need, then knuckle down and begin studying in earnest. Check your improvement regularly through the use of practice tests under real conditions. Above all, don't worry, panic, or give up. The key is perseverance!

Then, when you go to take the test, remain confident and remember how well you did on the practice tests. If you can score high enough on a practice test, then you can do the same on the real thing.

General Strategies

The most important thing you can do is to ignore your fears and jump into the test immediately. Do not be overwhelmed by any strange-sounding terms. You have to jump into the test like jumping into a pool—all at once is the easiest way.

Make Predictions

As you read and understand the question, try to guess what the answer will be. Remember that several of the answer choices are wrong, and once you begin reading them, your mind will immediately become cluttered with answer choices designed to throw you off. Your mind is typically the most focused immediately after you have read the question and digested its contents. If you can, try to predict what the correct answer will be. You may be surprised at what you can predict.

Quickly scan the choices and see if your prediction is in the listed answer choices. If it is, then you can be quite confident that you have the right answer. It still won't hurt to check the other answer choices, but most of the time, you've got it!

Answer the Question

It may seem obvious to only pick answer choices that answer the question, but the test writers can create some excellent answer choices that are wrong. Don't pick an answer just because it sounds right, or you believe it to be true. It MUST answer the question. Once you've made your selection, always go back and check it against the question and make sure that you didn't misread the question and that the answer choice does answer the question posed.

Benchmark

After you read the first answer choice, decide if you think it sounds correct or not. If it doesn't, move on to the next answer choice. If it does, mentally mark that answer choice. This doesn't mean that you've definitely selected it as your answer choice, it just means that it's the best you've seen thus far. Go ahead and read the next choice. If the next choice is worse than the one you've already selected, keep going to the next answer choice. If the next choice is better than the choice you've already selected, mentally mark the new answer choice as your best guess.

The first answer choice that you select becomes your standard. Every other answer choice must be benchmarked against that standard. That choice is correct until proven otherwise by another answer choice beating it out. Once you've decided that no other answer choice seems as good, do one final check to ensure that your answer choice answers the question posed.

Valid Information

Don't discount any of the information provided in the question. Every piece of information may be necessary to determine the correct answer. None of the information in the question is there to throw you off (while the answer choices will certainly have information to throw you off). If two seemingly unrelated topics are discussed, don't ignore either. You can be confident there is a relationship, or it wouldn't be included in the question, and you are probably going to have to determine what is that relationship to find the answer.

Avoid "Fact Traps"

Don't get distracted by a choice that is factually true. Your search is for the answer that answers the question. Stay focused and don't fall for an answer that is true but irrelevant. Always go back to the question and make sure you're choosing an answer that actually answers the question and is not just a true statement. An answer can be factually correct, but it MUST answer the question asked. Additionally, two answers can both be seemingly correct, so be sure to read all of the answer choices, and make sure that you get the one that BEST answers the question.

Milk the Question

Some of the questions may throw you completely off. They might deal with a subject you have not been exposed to, or one that you haven't reviewed in years. While your lack of knowledge about the subject will be a hindrance, the question itself can give you many clues that will help you find the correct answer. Read the question carefully and look for clues. Watch particularly for adjectives and nouns describing difficult terms or words that you don't recognize. Regardless of whether you completely understand a word or not, replacing it with a synonym, either provided or one you more familiar with, may help you to understand what the questions are asking. Rather than wracking your mind about specific detailed information concerning a difficult term or word, try to use mental substitutes that are easier to understand.

The Trap of Familiarity

Don't just choose a word because you recognize it. On difficult questions, you may not recognize a number of words in the answer choices. The test writers don't put "make-believe" words on the test, so don't think that just because you only recognize all the words in one answer choice that that answer choice must be correct. If you only recognize words in one answer choice, then focus on that one. Is it correct? Try your best to determine if it is correct. If it is, that's great. If not, eliminate it. Each word and answer choice you eliminate increases your chances of getting the question correct, even if you then have to guess among the unfamiliar choices.

Eliminate Answers

Eliminate choices as soon as you realize they are wrong. But be careful! Make sure you consider all of the possible answer choices. Just because one appears right, doesn't mean that the next one won't be even better! The test writers will usually put more than one good answer choice for every question, so read all of them. Don't worry if you are stuck between two that seem right. By getting down to just two remaining possible choices, your odds are now 50/50. Rather than wasting too much time, play the odds. You are guessing, but guessing wisely because you've been able to knock out some of the answer choices that you know are wrong. If you are eliminating choices and realize that the last answer choice you are left with is also obviously wrong, don't panic. Start over and consider each choice again. There may easily be something that you missed the first time and will realize on the second pass.

Tough Questions

If you are stumped on a problem or it appears too hard or too difficult, don't waste time. Move on! Remember though, if you can quickly check for obviously incorrect answer choices, your chances of guessing correctly are greatly improved. Before you completely give up, at least try to knock out a couple of possible answers. Eliminate what you can and then guess at the remaining answer choices before moving on.

Brainstorm

If you get stuck on a difficult question, spend a few seconds quickly brainstorming. Run through the complete list of possible answer choices. Look at each choice and ask yourself, "Could this answer the question satisfactorily?" Go through each answer choice and consider it independently of the others. By systematically going through all possibilities, you may find something that you would otherwise overlook. Remember though that when you get stuck, it's important to try to keep moving.

Read Carefully

Understand the problem. Read the question and answer choices carefully. Don't miss the question because you misread the terms. You have plenty of time to read each question thoroughly and make sure you understand what is being asked. Yet a happy medium must be attained, so don't waste too much time. You must read carefully, but efficiently.

Face Value

When in doubt, use common sense. Always accept the situation in the problem at face value. Don't read too much into it. These problems will not require you to make huge leaps of logic. The test writers aren't trying to throw you off with a cheap trick. If you have to go beyond creativity and make a leap of logic in order to have an answer choice answer the question, then you should look at the other answer choices. Don't overcomplicate the problem by creating theoretical relationships or explanations that will warp time or space. These are normal problems rooted in reality. It's just that the applicable relationship or explanation may not be readily apparent and you have to figure things out. Use your common sense to interpret anything that isn't clear.

Prefixes

If you're having trouble with a word in the question or answer choices, try dissecting it. Take advantage of every clue that the word might include. Prefixes and suffixes can be a huge help. Usually they allow you to determine a basic meaning. Pre- means before, post- means after, pro - is positive, de- is negative. From these prefixes and suffixes, you can get an idea of the general meaning of the word and try to put it into context. Beware though of any traps. Just because con- is the opposite of pro-, doesn't necessarily mean congress is the opposite of progress!

Hedge Phrases

Watch out for critical hedge phrases, led off with words such as "likely," "may," "can," "sometimes," "often," "almost," "mostly," "usually," "generally," "rarely," and "sometimes." Question writers insert these hedge phrases to cover every possibility. Often an answer choice will be wrong simply because it leaves no room for exception. Unless the situation calls for them, avoid answer choices that have definitive words like "exactly," and "always."

Switchback Words

Stay alert for "switchbacks." These are the words and phrases frequently used to alert you to shifts in thought. The most common switchback word is "but." Others include "although," "however," "nevertheless," "on the other hand," "even though," "while," "in spite of," "despite," and "regardless of."

New Information

Correct answer choices will rarely have completely new information included. Answer choices typically are straightforward reflections of the material asked about and will directly relate to the question. If a new piece of information is included in an answer choice that doesn't even seem to relate to the topic being asked about, then that answer choice is likely incorrect. All of the information needed to answer the question is usually provided for you in the question. You should not have to make guesses that are unsupported or choose answer choices that require unknown information that cannot be reasoned from what is given.

Time Management

On technical questions, don't get lost on the technical terms. Don't spend too much time on any one question. If you don't know what a term means, then odds are you aren't going to get much further since you don't have a dictionary. You should be able to immediately recognize whether or not you know a term. If you don't, work with the other clues that you have—the other answer choices and terms provided—but don't waste too much time trying to figure out a difficult term that you don't know.

Contextual Clues

Look for contextual clues. An answer can be right but not the correct answer. The contextual clues will help you find the answer that is most right and is correct. Understand the context in which a phrase or statement is made. This will help you make important distinctions.

Don't Panic

Panicking will not answer any questions for you; therefore, it isn't helpful. When you first see the question, if your mind goes blank, take a deep breath. Force yourself to mechanically go through the steps of solving the problem using the strategies you've learned.

Pace Yourself

Don't get clock fever. It's easy to be overwhelmed when you're looking at a page full of questions, your mind is full of random thoughts and feeling confused, and the clock is ticking down faster than you would like. Calm down and maintain the pace that you have set for yourself. As long as you are on track by monitoring your pace, you are guaranteed to have enough time for yourself. When you get to the last few minutes of the test, it may seem like you won't have enough time left, but if you only have as many questions as you should have left at that point, then you're right on track!

Answer Selection

The best way to pick an answer choice is to eliminate all of those that are wrong, until only one is left and confirm that is the correct answer. Sometimes though, an answer choice may immediately look right. Be careful! Take a second to make sure that the other choices are not equally obvious. Don't make a hasty mistake. There are only two times that you should stop before checking other answers. First is when you are positive that the answer choice you have selected is correct. Second is when time is almost out and you have to make a quick guess!

Check Your Work

Since you will probably not know every term listed and the answer to every question, it is important that you get credit for the ones that you do know. Don't miss any questions through careless mistakes. If at all possible, try to take a second to look back over your answer selection and make sure you've selected the correct answer choice and haven't made a costly careless mistake (such as marking an answer choice that you didn't mean to mark). The time it takes for this quick double check should more than pay for itself in caught mistakes.

Beware of Directly Quoted Answers

Sometimes an answer choice will repeat word for word a portion of the question or reference section. However, beware of such exact duplication. It may be a trap! More than likely, the correct choice will paraphrase or summarize a point, rather than being exactly the same wording.

Slang

Scientific sounding answers are better than slang ones. An answer choice that begins "To compare the outcomes..." is much more likely to be correct than one that begins "Because some people insisted..."

Extreme Statements

Avoid wild answers that throw out highly controversial ideas that are proclaimed as established fact. An answer choice that states the "process should be used in certain situations, if..." is much more likely to be correct than one that states the "process should be discontinued completely." The first is a calm rational statement and doesn't even make a definitive, uncompromising stance, using a hedge word "if" to provide wiggle room, whereas the second choice is a radical idea and far more extreme.

Answer Choice Families

When you have two or more answer choices that are direct opposites or parallels, one of them is usually the correct answer. For instance, if one answer choice states "x increases" and another answer choice states "x decreases" or "y increases," then those two or three answer choices are very similar in construction and fall into the same family of answer choices. A family of answer choices consists of two or three answer choices, very similar in construction, but often with directly opposite meanings. Usually the correct answer choice will be in that family of answer choices. The "odd man out" or answer choice that doesn't seem to fit the parallel construction of the other answer choices is more likely to be incorrect

Special Report: How to Overcome Test Anxiety

The very nature of tests caters to some level of anxiety, nervousness, or tension, just as we feel for any important event that occurs in our lives. A little bit of anxiety or nervousness can be a good thing. It helps us with motivation, and makes achievement just that much sweeter. However, too much anxiety can be a problem, especially if it hinders our ability to function and perform.

"Test anxiety," is the term that refers to the emotional reactions that some test-takers experience when faced with a test or exam. Having a fear of testing and exams is based upon a rational fear, since the test-taker's performance can shape the course of an academic career. Nevertheless, experiencing excessive fear of examinations will only interfere with the test-taker's ability to perform and chance to be successful.

There are a large variety of causes that can contribute to the development and sensation of test anxiety. These include, but are not limited to, lack of preparation and worrying about issues surrounding the test.

Lack of Preparation

Lack of preparation can be identified by the following behaviors or situations:

- Not scheduling enough time to study, and therefore cramming the night before the test or exam
- Managing time poorly, to create the sensation that there is not enough time to do everything
- Failing to organize the text information in advance, so that the study material consists of the entire text and not simply the pertinent information
- Poor overall studying habits

Worrying, on the other hand, can be related to both the test taker, or many other factors around him/her that will be affected by the results of the test. These include worrying about:

- Previous performances on similar exams, or exams in general
- How friends and other students are achieving
- The negative consequences that will result from a poor grade or failure

There are three primary elements to test anxiety. Physical components, which involve the same typical bodily reactions as those to acute anxiety (to be discussed below). Emotional factors have to do with fear or panic. Mental or cognitive issues concerning attention spans and memory abilities.

Physical Signals

There are many different symptoms of test anxiety, and these are not limited to mental and emotional strain. Frequently there are a range of physical signals that will let a test taker know that he/she is suffering from test anxiety. These bodily changes can include the following:

- Perspiring
- Sweaty palms
- Wet, trembling hands
- Nausea
- Dry mouth
- A knot in the stomach
- Headache
- Faintness
- Muscle tension
- Aching shoulders, back and neck
- Rapid heart beat
- Feeling too hot/cold

To recognize the sensation of test anxiety, a test-taker should monitor him/herself for the following sensations:

- The physical distress symptoms as listed above
- Emotional sensitivity, expressing emotional feelings such as the need to cry or laugh too much, or a sensation of anger or helplessness
- A decreased ability to think, causing the test-taker to blank out or have racing thoughts that are hard to organize or control.

Though most students will feel some level of anxiety when faced with a test or exam, the majority can cope with that anxiety and maintain it at a manageable level. However, those who cannot are faced with a very real and very serious condition, which can and should be controlled for the immeasurable benefit of this sufferer.

Naturally, these sensations lead to negative results for the testing experience. The most common effects of test anxiety have to do with nervousness and mental blocking.

Nervousness

Nervousness can appear in several different levels:

- The test-taker's difficulty, or even inability to read and understand the questions on the test
- The difficulty or inability to organize thoughts to a coherent form
- The difficulty or inability to recall key words and concepts relating to the testing questions (especially essays)
- The receipt of poor grades on a test, though the test material was well known by the test taker.
- Conversely, a person may also experience mental blocking, which involves:
- Blanking out on test questions
- Only remembering the correct answers to the questions when the test has already finished.

Fortunately for test anxiety sufferers, beating these feelings, to a large degree, has to do with proper preparation. When a test taker has a feeling of preparedness, then anxiety will be dramatically lessened.

The first step to resolving anxiety issues is to distinguish which of the two types of anxiety are being suffered. If the anxiety is a direct result of a lack of preparation, this should be considered a normal reaction, and the anxiety level (as opposed to the test results) shouldn't be anything to worry about. However, if, when adequately prepared, the test-taker still panics, blanks out, or seems to overreact, this is not a fully rational reaction. While this can be considered normal too, there are many ways to combat and overcome these effects.

Remember that anxiety cannot be entirely eliminated, however, there are ways to minimize it, to make the anxiety easier to manage. Preparation is one of the best ways to minimize test anxiety. Therefore the following techniques are wise in order to best fight off any anxiety that may want to build.

To begin with, try to avoid cramming before a test, whenever it is possible. By trying to memorize an entire term's worth of information in one day, you'll be shocking your system, and not giving yourself a very good chance to absorb the information. This is an easy path to anxiety, so for those who suffer from test anxiety, cramming should not even be considered an option.

Instead of cramming, work throughout the semester to combine all of the material which is presented throughout the semester, and work on it gradually as the course goes by, making sure to master the main concepts first, leaving minor details for a week or so before the test.

To study for the upcoming exam, be sure to pose questions that may be on the examination, to gauge the ability to answer them by integrating the ideas from your texts, notes and lectures, as well as any supplementary readings.

If it is truly impossible to cover all of the information that was covered in that particular term, concentrate on the most important portions, that can be covered very well. Learn these concepts as best as possible, so that when the test comes, a goal can be made to use these concepts as presentations of your knowledge.

In addition to study habits, changes in attitude are critical to beating a struggle with test anxiety. In fact, an improvement of the perspective over the entire test-taking experience can actually help a test taker to enjoy studying and therefore improve the overall experience. Be certain not to overemphasize the significance of the grade - know that the result of the test is neither a reflection of self worth, nor is it a measure of intelligence; one grade will not predict a person's future success.

To improve an overall testing outlook, the following steps should be tried:

- Keeping in mind that the most reasonable expectation for taking a test is to expect to try to demonstrate as much of what you know as you possibly can.
- Reminding ourselves that a test is only one test; this is not the only one, and there will be others.
- The thought of thinking of oneself in an irrational, all-or-nothing term should be avoided at all costs.
- A reward should be designated for after the test, so there's something to look forward to. Whether it be going to a movie, going out to eat, or simply visiting friends, schedule it in advance, and do it no matter what result is expected on the exam.

Test-takers should also keep in mind that the basics are some of the most important things, even beyond anti-anxiety techniques and studying. Never neglect the basic social, emotional and biological needs, in order to try to absorb information. In order to best achieve, these three factors must be held as just as important as the studying itself.

Study Steps

Remember the following important steps for studying:

- Maintain healthy nutrition and exercise habits. Continue both your recreational activities and social pass times. These both contribute to your physical and emotional well being.
- Be certain to get a good amount of sleep, especially the night before the test, because when you're overtired you are not able to perform to the best of your best ability.
- Keep the studying pace to a moderate level by taking breaks when they are needed, and varying the work whenever possible, to keep the mind fresh instead of getting bored.
- When enough studying has been done that all the material that can be learned has been learned, and the test taker is prepared for the test, stop studying and do something relaxing such as listening to music, watching a movie, or taking a warm bubble bath.

There are also many other techniques to minimize the uneasiness or apprehension that is experienced along with test anxiety before, during, or even after the examination. In fact, there are a great deal of things that can be done to stop anxiety from interfering with lifestyle and performance. Again, remember that anxiety will not be eliminated entirely, and it shouldn't be. Otherwise that "up" feeling for exams would not exist, and most of us depend on that sensation to perform better than usual. However, this anxiety has to be at a level that is manageable.

Of course, as we have just discussed, being prepared for the exam is half the battle right away. Attending all classes, finding out what knowledge will be expected on the exam, and knowing the exam schedules are easy steps to lowering anxiety. Keeping up with work will remove the need to cram, and efficient study habits will eliminate wasted time. Studying should be done in an ideal location for concentration, so that it is simple to become interested in the material and give it complete attention. A method such as SQ3R (Survey, Question, Read, Recite, Review) is a wonderful key to follow to make sure that the study habits are as effective as possible, especially in the case of learning from a textbook. Flashcards are great techniques for memorization. Learning to take good notes will mean that notes will be full of useful information, so that less sifting will need to be done to seek out what is pertinent for studying. Reviewing notes after class and then again on occasion will keep the information fresh in the mind. From notes that have been taken summary sheets and outlines can be made for simpler reviewing.

A study group can also be a very motivational and helpful place to study, as there will be a sharing of ideas, all of the minds can work together, to make sure that everyone understands, and the studying will be made more interesting because it will be a social occasion.

Basically, though, as long as the test-taker remains organized and self confident, with efficient study habits, less time will need to be spent studying, and higher grades will be achieved.

To become self confident, there are many useful steps. The first of these is "self talk." It has been shown through extensive research, that self-talk for students who suffer from test anxiety, should be well monitored, in order to make sure that it contributes to self confidence as opposed to sinking the student. Frequently the self talk of test-anxious students is negative or self-defeating, thinking that everyone else is smarter and faster, that they always mess up, and that if they don't do well, they'll fail the entire course. It is important to decreasing anxiety that awareness is made of self talk. Try writing any negative self thoughts and then disputing them with a positive statement instead. Begin self-encouragement as though it was a friend speaking. Repeat positive statements to help reprogram the mind to believing in successes instead of failures.

Helpful Techniques

Other extremely helpful techniques include:

- Self-visualization of doing well and reaching goals
- While aiming for an "A" level of understanding, don't try to "overprotect" by setting your expectations lower. This will only convince the mind to stop studying in order to meet the lower expectations.
- Don't make comparisons with the results or habits of other students. These are individual factors, and different things work for different people, causing different results.
- Strive to become an expert in learning what works well, and what can be done in order to improve. Consider collecting this data in a journal.
- Create rewards for after studying instead of doing things before studying that will only turn into avoidance behaviors.
- Make a practice of relaxing - by using methods such as progressive relaxation, self-hypnosis, guided imagery, etc - in order to make relaxation an automatic sensation.
- Work on creating a state of relaxed concentration so that concentrating will take on the focus of the mind, so that none will be wasted on worrying.
- Take good care of the physical self by eating well and getting enough sleep.
- Plan in time for exercise and stick to this plan.

Beyond these techniques, there are other methods to be used before, during and after the test that will help the test-taker perform well in addition to overcoming anxiety.

Before the exam comes the academic preparation. This involves establishing a study schedule and beginning at least one week before the actual date of the test. By doing this, the anxiety of not having enough time to study for the test will be automatically eliminated. Moreover, this will make the studying a much more effective experience, ensuring that the learning will be an easier process. This relieves much undue pressure on the test-taker.

Summary sheets, note cards, and flash cards with the main concepts and examples of these main concepts should be prepared in advance of the actual studying time. A topic should never be eliminated from this process. By omitting a topic because it isn't expected to be on the test is only setting up the test-taker for anxiety should it actually appear on the exam. Utilize the course syllabus for laying out the topics that should be studied. Carefully go over the notes that were made in class, paying special attention to any of the issues that the professor took special care to emphasize while lecturing in class. In the textbooks, use the chapter review, or if possible, the chapter tests, to begin your review.

It may even be possible to ask the instructor what information will be covered on the exam, or what the format of the exam will be (for example, multiple choice, essay, free form, true-false). Additionally, see if it is possible to find out how many questions will be on the test. If a review sheet or sample test has been offered by the professor, make good use of it, above anything else, for the preparation for the test. Another great resource for getting to know the examination is reviewing tests from previous semesters. Use these tests to review, and aim to achieve a 100%

score on each of the possible topics. With a few exceptions, the goal that you set for yourself is the highest one that you will reach.

Take all of the questions that were assigned as homework, and rework them to any other possible course material. The more problems reworked, the more skill and confidence will form as a result. When forming the solution to a problem, write out each of the steps. Don't simply do head work. By doing as many steps on paper as possible, much clarification and therefore confidence will be formed. Do this with as many homework problems as possible, before checking the answers. By checking the answer after each problem, a reinforcement will exist, that will not be on the exam. Study situations should be as exam-like as possible, to prime the test-taker's system for the experience. By waiting to check the answers at the end, a psychological advantage will be formed, to decrease the stress factor.

Another fantastic reason for not cramming is the avoidance of confusion in concepts, especially when it comes to mathematics. 8-10 hours of study will become one hundred percent more effective if it is spread out over a week or at least several days, instead of doing it all in one sitting. Recognize that the human brain requires time in order to assimilate new material, so frequent breaks and a span of study time over several days will be much more beneficial.

Additionally, don't study right up until the point of the exam. Studying should stop a minimum of one hour before the exam begins. This allows the brain to rest and put things in their proper order. This will also provide the time to become as relaxed as possible when going into the examination room. The test-taker will also have time to eat well and eat sensibly. Know that the brain needs food as much as the rest of the body. With enough food and enough sleep, as well as a relaxed attitude, the body and the mind are primed for success.

Avoid any anxious classmates who are talking about the exam. These students only spread anxiety, and are not worth sharing the anxious sentimentalities.

Before the test also involves creating a positive attitude, so mental preparation should also be a point of concentration. There are many keys to creating a positive attitude. Should fears become rushing in, make a visualization of taking the exam, doing well, and seeing an A written on the paper. Write out a list of affirmations that will bring a feeling of confidence, such as "I am doing well in my English class," "I studied well and know my material," "I enjoy this class." Even if the affirmations aren't believed at first, it sends a positive message to the subconscious which will result in an alteration of the overall belief system, which is the system that creates reality.

If a sensation of panic begins, work with the fear and imagine the very worst! Work through the entire scenario of not passing the test, failing the entire course, and dropping out of school, followed by not getting a job, and pushing a shopping cart through the dark alley where you'll live. This will place things into perspective! Then, practice deep breathing and create a visualization of the opposite situation - achieving an "A" on the exam, passing the entire course, receiving the degree at a graduation ceremony.

On the day of the test, there are many things to be done to ensure the best results, as well as the most calm outlook. The following stages are suggested in order to maximize test-taking potential:

- Begin the examination day with a moderate breakfast, and avoid any coffee or beverages with caffeine if the test taker is prone to jitters. Even people who are used to managing caffeine can feel jittery or light-headed when it is taken on a test day.

- Attempt to do something that is relaxing before the examination begins. As last minute cramming clouds the mastering of overall concepts, it is better to use this time to create a calming outlook.
- Be certain to arrive at the test location well in advance, in order to provide time to select a location that is away from doors, windows and other distractions, as well as giving enough time to relax before the test begins.
- Keep away from anxiety generating classmates who will upset the sensation of stability and relaxation that is being attempted before the exam.
- Should the waiting period before the exam begins cause anxiety, create a self-distraction by reading a light magazine or something else that is relaxing and simple.

During the exam itself, read the entire exam from beginning to end, and find out how much time should be allotted to each individual problem. Once writing the exam, should more time be taken for a problem, it should be abandoned, in order to begin another problem. If there is time at the end, the unfinished problem can always be returned to and completed.

Read the instructions very carefully - twice - so that unpleasant surprises won't follow during or after the exam has ended.

When writing the exam, pretend that the situation is actually simply the completion of homework within a library, or at home. This will assist in forming a relaxed atmosphere, and will allow the brain extra focus for the complex thinking function.

Begin the exam with all of the questions with which the most confidence is felt. This will build the confidence level regarding the entire exam and will begin a quality momentum. This will also create encouragement for trying the problems where uncertainty resides.

Going with the "gut instinct" is always the way to go when solving a problem. Second guessing should be avoided at all costs. Have confidence in the ability to do well.

For essay questions, create an outline in advance that will keep the mind organized and make certain that all of the points are remembered. For multiple choice, read every answer, even if the correct one has been spotted - a better one may exist.

Continue at a pace that is reasonable and not rushed, in order to be able to work carefully. Provide enough time to go over the answers at the end, to check for small errors that can be corrected.

Should a feeling of panic begin, breathe deeply, and think of the feeling of the body releasing sand through its pores. Visualize a calm, peaceful place, and include all of the sights, sounds and sensations of this image. Continue the deep breathing, and take a few minutes to continue this with closed eyes. When all is well again, return to the test.

If a "blanking" occurs for a certain question, skip it and move on to the next question. There will be time to return to the other question later. Get everything done that can be done, first, to guarantee all the grades that can be compiled, and to build all of the confidence possible. Then return to the weaker questions to build the marks from there. Remember, one's own reality can be created, so as long as the belief is there, success will follow. And remember: anxiety can happen later, right now, there's an exam to be written!

After the examination is complete, whether there is a feeling for a good grade or a bad grade, don't dwell on the exam, and be certain to follow through on the reward that was promised...and enjoy it! Don't dwell on any mistakes that have been made, as there is nothing that can be done at this point anyway. Additionally, don't begin to study for the next test right away. Do something relaxing for a while, and let the mind relax and prepare itself to begin absorbing information again.

From the results of the exam - both the grade and the entire experience, be certain to learn from what has gone on. Perfect studying habits and work some more on confidence in order to make the next examination experience even better than the last one.

Learn to avoid places where openings occurred for laziness, procrastination and day dreaming.

Use the time between this exam and the next one to better learn to relax, even learning to relax on cue, so that any anxiety can be controlled during the next exam. Learn how to relax the body. Slouch in your chair if that helps. Tighten and then relax all of the different muscle groups, one group at a time, beginning with the feet and then working all the way up to the neck and face. This will ultimately relax the muscles more than they were to begin with. Learn how to breathe deeply and comfortably, and focus on this breathing going in and out as a relaxing thought. With every exhale, repeat the word "relax."

As common as test anxiety is, it is very possible to overcome it. Make yourself one of the test-takers who overcome this frustrating hindrance.

Special Report: Retaking the Test: What Are Your Chances at Improving Your Score?

After going through the experience of taking a major test, many test takers feel that once is enough. The test usually comes during a period of transition in the test taker's life, and taking the test is only one of a series of important events. With so many distractions and conflicting recommendations, it may be difficult for a test taker to rationally determine whether or not he should retake the test after viewing his scores.

The importance of the test usually only adds to the burden of the retake decision. However, don't be swayed by emotion. There a few simple questions that you can ask yourself to guide you as you try to determine whether a retake would improve your score:

1. What went wrong? Why wasn't your score what you expected?

Can you point to a single factor or problem that you feel caused the low score? Were you sick on test day? Was there an emotional upheaval in your life that caused a distraction? Were you late for the test or not able to use the full time allotment? If you can point to any of these specific, individual problems, then a retake should definitely be considered.

2. Is there enough time to improve?

Many problems that may show up in your score report may take a lot of time for improvement. A deficiency in a particular math skill may require weeks or months of tutoring and studying to improve. If you have enough time to improve an identified weakness, then a retake should definitely be considered.

3. How will additional scores be used? Will a score average, highest score, or most recent score be used?

Different test scores may be handled completely differently. If you've taken the test multiple times, sometimes your highest score is used, sometimes your average score is computed and used, and sometimes your most recent score is used. Make sure you understand what method will be used to evaluate your scores, and use that to help you determine whether a retake should be considered.

4. Are my practice test scores significantly higher than my actual test score?

If you have taken a lot of practice tests and are consistently scoring at a much higher level than your actual test score, then you should consider a retake. However, if you've taken five practice tests and only one of your scores was higher than your actual test score, or if your practice test scores were only slightly higher than your actual test score, then it is unlikely that you will significantly increase your score.

5. Do I need perfect scores or will I be able to live with this score? Will this score still allow me to follow my dreams?

What kind of score is acceptable to you? Is your current score "good enough?" Do you have to have a certain score in order to pursue the future of your dreams? If you won't be happy with your current score, and there's no way that you could live with it, then you should consider a retake. However, don't get your hopes up. If you are looking for significant improvement, that may or may not be possible. But if you won't be happy otherwise, it is at least worth the effort.

Remember that there are other considerations. To achieve your dream, it is likely that your grades may also be taken into account. A great test score is usually not the only thing necessary to succeed. Make sure that you aren't overemphasizing the importance of a high test score.

Furthermore, a retake does not always result in a higher score. Some test takers will score lower on a retake, rather than higher. One study shows that one-fourth of test takers will achieve a significant improvement in test score, while one-sixth of test takers will actually show a decrease. While this shows that most test takers will improve, the majority will only improve their scores a little and a retake may not be worth the test taker's effort.

Finally, if a test is taken only once and is considered in the added context of good grades on the part of a test taker, the person reviewing the grades and scores may be tempted to assume that the test taker just had a bad day while taking the test, and may discount the low test score in favor of the high grades. But if the test is retaken and the scores are approximately the same, then the validity of the low scores are only confirmed. Therefore, a retake could actually hurt a test taker by definitely bracketing a test taker's score ability to a limited range.

How to Overcome Your Fear of Math

The word *math* is enough to strike fear into most hearts. How many of us have memories of sitting through confusing lectures, wrestling over mind-numbing homework, or taking tests that still seem incomprehensible even after hours of study? Years after graduation, many still shudder at these memories.

The fact is, math is not just a classroom subject. It has real-world implications that you face every day, whether you realize it or not. This may be balancing your monthly budget, deciding how many supplies to buy for a project, or simply splitting a meal check with friends. The idea of daily confrontations with math can be so paralyzing that some develop a condition known as *math anxiety*.

But you do NOT need to be paralyzed by this anxiety! In fact, while you may have thought all your life that you're not good at math, or that your brain isn't wired to understand it, the truth is that you may have been conditioned to think this way. From your earliest school days, the way you were taught affected the way you viewed different subjects. And the way math has been taught has changed.

Several decades ago, there was a shift in American math classrooms. The focus changed from traditional problem-solving to a conceptual view of topics, de-emphasizing the importance of learning the basics and building on them. The solid foundation necessary for math progression and confidence was undermined. Math became more of a vague concept than a concrete idea. Today, it is common to think of math, not as a straightforward system, but as a mysterious, complicated method that can't be fully understood unless you're a genius.

This is why you may still have nightmares about being called on to answer a difficult problem in front of the class. Math anxiety is a very real, though unnecessary, fear.

Math anxiety may begin with a single class period. Let's say you missed a day in 6th grade math and never quite understood the concept that was taught while you were gone. Since math is cumulative, with each new concept building on past ones, this could very well affect the rest of your math career. Without that one day's knowledge, it will be difficult to understand any other concepts that link to it. Rather than realizing that you're just missing one key piece, you may begin to believe that you're simply not capable of understanding math.

This belief can change the way you approach other classes, career options, and everyday life experiences, if you become anxious at the thought that math might be required. A student who loves science may choose a different path of study upon realizing that multiple math classes will be required for a degree. An aspiring medical student may hesitate at the thought of going through the necessary math classes. For some this anxiety escalates into a more extreme state known as *math phobia*.

Math anxiety is challenging to address because it is rooted deeply and may come from a variety of causes: an embarrassing moment in class, a teacher who did not explain concepts well and contributed to a shaky foundation, or a failed test that contributed to the belief of math failure.

These causes add up over time, encouraged by society's popular view that math is hard and unpleasant. Eventually a person comes to firmly believe that he or she is simply bad at math. This belief makes it difficult to grasp new concepts or even remember old ones. Homework and test grades begin to slip, which only confirms the belief. The poor performance is not due to lack of ability but is caused by math anxiety.

Math anxiety is an emotional issue, not a lack of intelligence. But when it becomes deeply rooted, it can become more than just an emotional problem. Physical symptoms appear. Blood pressure may rise and heartbeat may quicken at the sight of a math problem – or even the thought of math! This fear leads to a mental block. When someone with math anxiety is asked to perform a calculation, even a basic problem can seem overwhelming and impossible. The emotional and physical response to the thought of math prevents the brain from working through it logically.

The more this happens, the more a person's confidence drops, and the more math anxiety is generated. This vicious cycle must be broken!

The first step in breaking the cycle is to go back to very beginning and make sure you really understand the basics of how math works and why it works. It is not enough to memorize rules for multiplication and division. If you don't know WHY these rules work, your foundation will be shaky and you will be at risk of developing a phobia. Understanding mathematical concepts not only promotes confidence and security, but allows you to build on this understanding for new concepts. Additionally, you can solve unfamiliar problems using familiar concepts and processes.

Why is it that students in other countries regularly outperform American students in math? The answer likely boils down to a couple of things: the foundation of mathematical conceptual understanding and societal perception. While students in the US are not expected to *like* or *get* math, in many other nations, students are expected not only to understand math but also to excel at it.

Changing the American view of math that leads to math anxiety is a monumental task. It requires changing the training of teachers nationwide, from kindergarten through high school, so that they learn to teach the *why* behind math and to combat the wrong math views that students may develop. It also involves changing the stigma associated with math, so that it is no longer viewed as unpleasant and incomprehensible. While these are necessary changes, they are challenging and will take time. But in the meantime, math anxiety is not irreversible – it can be faced and defeated, one person at a time.

False Beliefs

One reason math anxiety has taken such hold is that several false beliefs have been created and shared until they became widely accepted. Some of these unhelpful beliefs include the following:

- *There is only one way to solve a math problem.* In the same way that you can choose from different driving routes and still arrive at the same house, you can solve a math problem using different methods and still find the correct answer. A person who understands the reasoning behind math calculations may be able to look at an unfamiliar concept and find the right answer, just by applying logic to the knowledge they already have. This approach may be different than what is taught in the classroom, but it is still valid. Unfortunately, even many teachers view math as a subject where the best course of action is to memorize

- 115 -

the rule or process for each problem rather than as a place for students to exercise logic and creativity in finding a solution.

- *Many people don't have a mind for math.* A person who has struggled due to poor teaching or math anxiety may falsely believe that he or she doesn't have the mental capacity to grasp mathematical concepts. Most of the time, this is false. Many people find that when they are relieved of their math anxiety, they have more than enough brainpower to understand math.
- *Men are naturally better at math than women.* Even though research has shown this to be false, many young women still avoid math careers and classes because of their belief that their math abilities are inferior. Many girls have come to believe that math is a male skill and have given up trying to understand or enjoy it.
- *Counting aids are bad.* Something like counting on your fingers or drawing out a problem to visualize it may be frowned on as childish or a crutch, but these devices can help you get a tangible understanding of a problem or a concept.

Sadly, many students buy into these ideologies at an early age. A young girl who enjoys math class may be conditioned to think that she doesn't actually have the brain for it because math is for boys, and may turn her energies to other pursuits, permanently closing the door on a wide range of opportunities. A child who finds the right answer but doesn't follow the teacher's method may believe that he is doing it wrong and isn't good at math. A student who never had a problem with math before may have a poor teacher and become confused, yet believe that the problem is because she doesn't have a mathematical mind.

Students who have bought into these erroneous beliefs quickly begin to add their own anxieties, adapting them to their own personal situations:

- *I'll never use this in real life.* A huge number of people wrongly believe that math is irrelevant outside the classroom. By adopting this mindset, they are handicapping themselves for a life in a mathematical world, as well as limiting their career choices. When they are inevitably faced with real-world math, they are conditioning themselves to respond with anxiety.
- *I'm not quick enough.* While timed tests and quizzes, or even simply comparing yourself with other students in the class, can lead to this belief, speed is not an indicator of skill level. A person can work very slowly yet understand at a deep level.
- *If I can understand it, it's too easy.* People with a low view of their own abilities tend to think that if they are able to grasp a concept, it must be simple. They cannot accept the idea that they are capable of understanding math. This belief will make it harder to learn, no matter how intelligent they are.
- *I just can't learn this.* An overwhelming number of people think this, from young children to adults, and much of the time it is simply not true. But this mindset can turn into a self-fulfilling prophecy that keeps you from exercising and growing your math ability.

The good news is, each of these myths can be debunked. For most people, they are based on emotion and psychology, NOT on actual ability! It will take time, effort, and the desire to change, but change is possible. Even if you have spent years thinking that you don't have the capability to understand math, it is not too late to uncover your true ability and find relief from the anxiety that surrounds math.

Math Strategies

It is important to have a plan of attack to combat math anxiety. There are many useful strategies for pinpointing the fears or myths and eradicating them:

Go back to the basics. For most people, math anxiety stems from a poor foundation. You may think that you have a complete understanding of addition and subtraction, or even decimals and percentages, but make absolutely sure. Learning math is different from learning other subjects. For example, when you learn history, you study various time periods and places and events. It may be important to memorize dates or find out about the lives of famous people. When you move from US history to world history, there will be some overlap, but a large amount of the information will be new. Mathematical concepts, on the other hand, are very closely linked and highly dependent on each other. It's like climbing a ladder – if a rung is missing from your understanding, it may be difficult or impossible for you to climb any higher, no matter how hard you try. So go back and make sure your math foundation is strong. This may mean taking a remedial math course, going to a tutor to work through the shaky concepts, or just going through your old homework to make sure you really understand it.

Speak the language. Math has a large vocabulary of terms and phrases unique to working problems. Sometimes these are completely new terms, and sometimes they are common words, but are used differently in a math setting. If you can't speak the language, it will be very difficult to get a thorough understanding of the concepts. It's common for students to think that they don't understand math when they simply don't understand the vocabulary. The good news is that this is fairly easy to fix. Brushing up on any terms you aren't quite sure of can help bring the rest of the concepts into focus.

Check your anxiety level. When you think about math, do you feel nervous or uncomfortable? Do you struggle with feelings of inadequacy, even on concepts that you know you've already learned? It's important to understand your specific math anxieties, and what triggers them. When you catch yourself falling back on a false belief, mentally replace it with the truth. Don't let yourself believe that you can't learn, or that struggling with a concept means you'll never understand it. Instead, remind yourself of how much you've already learned and dwell on that past success. Visualize grasping the new concept, linking it to your old knowledge, and moving on to the next challenge. Also, learn how to manage anxiety when it arises. There are many techniques for coping with the irrational fears that rise to the surface when you enter the math classroom. This may include controlled breathing, replacing negative thoughts with positive ones, or visualizing success. Anxiety interferes with your ability to concentrate and absorb information, which in turn contributes to greater anxiety. If you can learn how to regain control of your thinking, you will be better able to pay attention, make progress, and succeed!

Don't go it alone. Like any deeply ingrained belief, math anxiety is not easy to eradicate. And there is no need for you to wrestle through it on your own. It will take time, and many people find that speaking with a counselor or psychiatrist helps. They can help you develop strategies for responding to anxiety and overcoming old ideas. Additionally, it can be very helpful to take a short course or seek out a math tutor to help you find and fix the missing rungs on your ladder and make sure that you're ready to progress to the next level. You can also find a number of math aids online: courses that will teach you mental devices for figuring out problems, how to get the most out of your math classes, etc.

Check your math attitude. No matter how much you want to learn and overcome your anxiety, you'll have trouble if you still have a negative attitude toward math. If you think it's too hard, or just have general feelings of dread about math, it will be hard to learn and to break through the anxiety. Work on cultivating a positive math attitude. Remind yourself that math is not just a hurdle to be cleared, but a valuable asset. When you view math with a positive attitude, you'll be much more likely to understand and even enjoy it. This is something you must do for yourself. You may find it helpful to visit with a counselor. Your tutor, friends, and family may cheer you on in your endeavors. But your greatest asset is yourself. You are inside your own mind – tell yourself what you need to hear. Relive past victories. Remind yourself that you are capable of understanding math. Root out any false beliefs that linger and replace them with positive truths. Even if it doesn't feel true at first, it will begin to affect your thinking and pave the way for a positive, anxiety-free mindset.

Aside from these general strategies, there are a number of specific practical things you can do to begin your journey toward overcoming math anxiety. Something as simple as learning a new note-taking strategy can change the way you approach math and give you more confidence and understanding. New study techniques can also make a huge difference.

Math anxiety leads to bad habits. If it causes you to be afraid of answering a question in class, you may gravitate toward the back row. You may be embarrassed to ask for help. And you may procrastinate on assignments, which leads to rushing through them at the last moment when it's too late to get a better understanding. It's important to identify your negative behaviors and replace them with positive ones:

Prepare ahead of time. Read the lesson before you go to class. Being exposed to the topics that will be covered in class ahead of time, even if you don't understand them perfectly, is extremely helpful in increasing what you retain from the lecture. Do your homework and, if you're still shaky, go over some extra problems. The key to a solid understanding of math is practice.

Sit front and center. When you can easily see and hear, you'll understand more, and you'll avoid the distractions of other students if no one is in front of you. Plus, you're more likely to be sitting with students who are positive and engaged, rather than others with math anxiety. Let their positive math attitude rub off on you.

Ask questions in class and out. If you don't understand something, just ask. If you need a more in-depth explanation, the teacher may need to work with you outside of class, but often it's a simple concept you don't quite understand, and a single question may clear it up. If you wait, you may not be able to follow the rest of the day's lesson. For extra help, most professors have office hours outside of class when you can go over concepts one-on-one to clear up any uncertainties. Additionally, there may be a *math lab* or study session you can attend for homework help. Take advantage of this.

Review. Even if you feel that you've fully mastered a concept, review it periodically to reinforce it. Going over an old lesson has several benefits: solidifying your understanding, giving you a confidence boost, and even giving some new insights into material that you're currently learning! Don't let yourself get rusty. That can lead to problems with learning later concepts.

Teaching Tips

While the math student's mindset is the most crucial to overcoming math anxiety, it is also important for others to adjust their math attitudes. Teachers and parents have an enormous influence on how students relate to math. They can either contribute to math confidence or math anxiety.

As a parent or teacher, it is very important to convey a positive math attitude. Retelling horror stories of your own bad experience with math will contribute to a new generation of math anxiety. Even if you don't share your experiences, others will be able to sense your fears and may begin to believe them.

Even a careless comment can have a big impact, so watch for phrases like "He's not good at math" or "I never liked math." You are a crucial role model, and your children or students will unconsciously adopt your mindset. Give them a positive example to follow. Rather than teaching them to fear the math world before they even know it, teach them about all its potential and excitement.

Work to present math as an integral, beautiful, and understandable part of life. Encourage creativity in solving problems. Watch for false beliefs and dispel them. Cross the lines between subjects: integrate history, English, and music with math. Show students how math is used every day, and how the entire world is based on mathematical principles, from the pull of gravity to the shape of seashells. Instead of letting students see math as a necessary evil, direct them to view it as an imaginative, beautiful art form – an art form that they are capable of mastering and using.

Don't give too narrow a view of math. It is more than just numbers. Yes, working problems and learning formulas is a large part of classroom math. But don't let the teaching stop there. Teach students about the everyday implications of math. Show them how nature works according to the laws of mathematics, and take them outside to make discoveries of their own. Expose them to math-related careers by inviting visiting speakers, asking students to do research and presentations, and learning students' interests and aptitudes on a personal level.

Demonstrate the importance of math. Many people see math as nothing more than a required stepping stone to their degree, a nuisance with no real usefulness. Teach students that algebra is used every day in managing their bank accounts, in following recipes, and in scheduling the day's events. Show them how learning to do geometric proofs helps them to develop logical thinking, an invaluable life skill. Let them see that math surrounds them and is integrally linked to their daily lives: that weather predictions are based on math, that math was used to design cars and other machines, etc. Most of all, give them the tools to use math to enrich their lives.

Make math as tangible as possible. Use visual aids and objects that can be touched. It is much easier to grasp a concept when you can hold it in your hands and manipulate it, rather than just listening to the lecture. Encourage math outside of the classroom. The real world is full of measuring, counting, and calculating, so let students participate in this. Keep your eyes open for numbers and patterns to discuss. Talk about how scores are calculated in sports games and how far apart plants are placed in a garden row for maximum growth. Build the mindset that math is a normal and interesting part of daily life.

Finally, find math resources that help to build a positive math attitude. There are a number of books that show math as fascinating and exciting while teaching important concepts, for example: *The*

Math Curse; A Wrinkle in Time; The Phantom Tollbooth; and *Fractals, Googols and Other Mathematical Tales.* You can also find a number of online resources: math puzzles and games, videos that show math in nature, and communities of math enthusiasts. On a local level, students can compete in a variety of math competitions with other schools or join a math club.

The student who experiences math as exciting and interesting is unlikely to suffer from math anxiety. Going through life without this handicap is an immense advantage and opens many doors that others have closed through their fear.

Self-Check

Whether you suffer from math anxiety or not, chances are that you have been exposed to some of the false beliefs mentioned above. Now is the time to check yourself for any errors you may have accepted. Do you think you're not wired for math? Or that you don't need to understand it since you're not planning on a math career? Do you think math is just too difficult for the average person?

Find the errors you've taken to heart and replace them with positive thinking. Are you capable of learning math? Yes! Can you control your anxiety? Yes! These errors will resurface from time to time, so be watchful. Don't let others with math anxiety influence you or sway your confidence. If you're having trouble with a concept, find help. Don't let it discourage you!

Create a plan of attack for defeating math anxiety and sharpening your skills. Do some research and decide if it would help you to take a class, get a tutor, or find some online resources to fine-tune your knowledge. Make the effort to get good nutrition, hydration, and sleep so that you are operating at full capacity. Remind yourself daily that you are skilled and that anxiety does not control you. Your mind is capable of so much more than you know. Give it the tools it needs to grow and thrive.

Additional Bonus Material

Due to our efforts to try to keep this book to a manageable length, we've created a link that will give you access to all of your additional bonus material.

Please visit http://www.mometrix.com/bonus948/iseelower to access the information.

80231880R00075

Made in the USA
San Bernardino, CA
24 June 2018